I0140280

The Business of Game

Sex and Money
The Common Denominator
Between Classes in America

The Business of Game

Published by D. Supreem Young

Copyright 2009 by D. Supreem Young

All rights reserved under International and Pan American copyright Conventions. Published in the United States by D. "Supreem" Young

No part of this book may be reproduced or utilized in any form or by any means, electronic or mechanical, including photocopying, recording or by information storage system, without permission in writing from the publisher. Inquires should be addressed to Permissions Department, at 2435 East North Street, Suite 301, Greenville S.C. 29615

www.thebusinessofgame.com or thebusinessofgame@yahoo.com

Library of Congress Control Number 2009904827

ISBN 978-0-578-02155-3

Manufactured in the United States of America

THE BUSINESS OF GAME
www.thebusinessofgame.com
thebusinessofgame@yahoo.com

"THE BUSINESS OF GAME"

is a movement that every Business man, "Player", Hustler and Civilian should be aware of, This book introduces you to, places and things that your parents didn't tell you about which makes it one of the most simple but yet so complicated books on the market.

Be Honest, Be Loyal, Adapt, Believe in Yourself
This book is dedicated to all the females in my life, those that wrecked and tried to ruin it, and those that helped me recover, rebuild and over come, but most especially to my dear mother and grandmother Eva, and my deceased great-grand mother; Lilly R.B. Sanders.

Society's public response would have you believe that sex for money is not accepted within America but the reality is; sex for money is accepted in America without acceptance.

Some of the names mentioned in "situations" may have been altered to protect the privacies of families.

Acknowledgements

Thanks to the following people involved with my motivation and inspiration: Hubert B. Sanders, Herbert Young, Thurston Sanders, William Young, Harold Kline and family, James Werts, Bernard Lindsey, Tony Bailey, Carolyn Young, Cassandra Young (you're still "Poochie"), Paige Cheeks for typing and edit, Jessica Love, Julian L.D. Shabazz, David L. Shabazz, Travius Fisher, Danny, Ray, Lamar "Fat Frank", Jamal, "Ribby", "Grand" , "Quick" , "Heavy", Mr. Dendy, Costell Little, Lorenzo Evans, Marvin Rice, Bo Bo, Billy Leopard   Wayne Copeland Fred Tyler (TOPS in Photography), Isaac Freeman (Pure Work Entertainment), Cleophus Moore, Wade and Barbara Jean Barr, "Stonewall" Craig   Rev. Anthony Simms,   Rev. McLamor, Curtis Nance, Bob ("Snake"), Kendrick, Sammy, D. J. Quick Silva (Baltimore/ D.C.), models "Jordan", and Chloe, "Diamond", "Honey", Peaches, Tweet, "Fantasy Island", "Mr. Lucky's", "Trophy Club", "Magic City", Club Roc-Bottum and the hundreds of people, places and experiences has been priceless in providing information on the secrets of

"THE BUSINESS OF GAME"

Table of Contents

Introduction

Now that you are holding this book, "The Business of Game" ask yourself; have you ever been serious about your life and the life of your partner but your partner didn't take their life or your life serious? A lot of people believe that if they do the right thing and treat people good that they will never become the victim of a player, gold digger, prostitute, call girl, pimp, house wives and any other person with deceitful tactics to gain money and possessions will fit under the umbrella title "BOOTLEGGERS".

There has been a saying "THE GAME DOESN'T CHANGE, ONLY THE PLAYERS". Well "The Business of Game" will prove just the opposite. "The Game" is over, the, younger generation of "players" (sorry) participants along with today's economy really has the game in a "strangle hold" in fact, sex for money has never been a game and has always been a business. "Tricks" (men) must protect themselves when being involved with the sex business. There are losers at the end of a game. To have sex with someone now-a-days is the most important business decision a person can make today. Sex with a person today comes to a negative total for most men. Men have been and are still paying for sex by losing their jobs, family, careers, finances, position, status as well as freedom. Sex was a business and is still a business. The "Business of Game" continues for men through Alimony, Palimony and Child support.

Growing up, I witness men loosing lifelong possessions and accomplishments behind the actions or responses to females. For the early part of my life, I never really understood what the terms "Player", "Hustler" or "Game" was all about. At the age of 13, I got my first girlfriend. She happened to be one of the prettiest girls in the town. I notice more girls paying attention to me with her as my girl. By 17 years old, I was in high school with a different girlfriend yet, one of the prettiest in the school. By this time, I didn't just notice girls liking me but I noticed them being disrespectful towards my girlfriend in order to get my attention. At the time I was surprised because I had been taught as a little boy to respect girls and I always assumed that they were made with "sugar, spice and everything nice" noticing the disrespect that females show to one another introduced me to another world. That world came in the form of college drugs, money, girls, girls, girls and sex. With money, cars, and known to date the prettiest girls, females was still willing to date (sleep with) me. This is when I learned and decided to be honest with women about most of the things that guys normally lie about such as: do you have a girlfriend? "Yes!" Do you only want sex from me? "Yes, for now! And we can see if the friendship matures. You wouldn't buy a new or used car before you test drive it; that would not be fair to neither of you." By being honest with females I have more than doubled my scoring percentage with ladies from many "walks of life" (backgrounds).

After years of learning, experiencing, managing, owning clubs, promoting exotic dancers and teaching The Business (game) to up and coming "Players", Hustlers, and business people. I have finally been convinced (Paid) to put The Business of Game on paper. Lying has always been a part of the "game" but you profit more once you incorporate witty, unexpected honesty. Example: A female ask me the question "what is it about me did I like and why did I enjoy spending time with her." I was in no mood to give a verbal massage even though, I knew she needed a ego boost at the time, I replied; "I'm a shame to admit it but I like you for a selfish reason, I like you for how you make me feel, you really lift my spirits and I appreciate knowing that I have you on my team. I get a genuine security from being with you that isn't easily provided". That made her day; she made it her duty to please me and to become my sponsor.

Supreem

Chapter 1

Confessions of "Con"sessions

As he "diddy-bopped" from his brand new CLS 550 Mercedes Benz, his teeth symmetrically perfect and white, his spoken and unspoken words was like a chant of charm. His Giorgio Armani suit was 100% imported raw silk his tie was matching his ostrich skin belt and the finest ostrich skin boots that money could buy. His platinum crown tooth glistened under the afternoon sun just as much as his platinum neck piece that matched his platinum and diamond rings. Meanwhile, the most beautiful women in the city hurriedly stepped to him, acting as adolescent teenage groupies as they awaited his commands... Deception, lies and corruption is his games, cons, sleaze and depravity is his middle names. Fraud, hoaxes and trickery is his call to fame. He could sell snake oil to a snake oil salesman. Yes that was Reverend Taylor who like a number of other ministers, are ruining the foundation of families and diminishing the fabric of the Christian community.

The word **Congregation** is commonly referred to as a religious group or community that follows a certain order or rule. The prefix for congregation is **Con,** which is normally associated being involved with a swindle as if to cheat or persuade under false pretense, also is associated with a person serving or have served a prison sentence.

8

REV. Jesse Louis Jackson

Rev. Jackson was born Jesse Louis Burns in Greenville, South Carolina, he became Jesse L. Jackson at the age of 14 after taking on his step-fathers name. Rev. Jackson went to the University of Illinois on a football scholarship. Jesse Jackson had issues about the quarterback position and transferred to North Carolina A&T University after being placed on academic probation by the end of his second semester at the University of Illinois. Although Jackson transferred in hopes of a better life, he did not graduate from NC A&T. Jackson decided to become a preacher. He attended the Chicago Theological Seminary, changing his mind shortly after this decision; he dropped out of seminary school. In 1968, he decided he would become a minister after all; by knowing the right people, he was ordained without a Theological degree. In 1990 he received an honorary doctorate from Chicago and a Master's Degree in Divinity was rewarded to him in 2000 due to his previous life experiences.

Rev. Jackson participated in a few marches in Alabama and happened to meet and work along side Dr. Martin Luther King Jr. He was also involved in many other organizations like "The Rainbow Push Organization". Rev. Jackson also worked with Ralph Abernathy, who was appointed by Dr. King to head the National SCLC in 1971. Rev. Jackson didn't seem to work well with Ralph Abernathy, as a result of this; he was out of a "GIG". Like any good Business man, Hustler, Minister or "Con", he knew that he had to bring in some form of income. If you have ever played any type of sport or been a member of a gym, you would often hear the coach or instructor say "hustle" that means to break a sweat. Less than a month from his break with Ralph Abernathy, Rev. Jackson had hustled and used his mouth piece to gather enough support (money) to birth the Rainbow coalition. By 1983, Rev. Jackson had been a success at getting a few American hostages released (most good "cons" are very persuasive). He was later invited to the White House by President Ronald W. Reagan. Shortly afterwards, Rev. Jackson had the nerve to announce to the world that he would be running for President of the United States of America in 1984. Well, Rev. Jackson ran and was defeated. By 2006, the Rainbow Coalition had merged with Operation Push Organization and became known as the Rainbow Push Organization.

Rev. Jackson has been known for enjoying the spotlight and having the need for attention. He had another shot at the limelight in 2006 when a stripper accused three Duke University athletes of a sex "scandal" or "scam". The Duke University Lacrosse players were found innocent and cleared of charges. Because Rev. Jackson had previously committed the finances of the Rainbow/Push Coalition to pay the rest of the accusers' college tuition, no matter the outcome of the case, this still had to be done. It also appeared that the young lady (accuser) had more "game" (Business) about her than Rev. Jackson.

Still sweating and hustling in 2006, the comedian Michael Richards used the "N" word and eventually met face to face with Rev. Jackson to publicly apologize. Rev. Jackson accepted Richard's apology. I have never really understood who allowed Rev. Jackson to be the representative of African Americans. Michael Richards has suffered as a result of his comments and probably had an affect on his business affairs. I believe that Jesse Jackson should sit face to face with Michael Richards and reverse the apology because of his hypocritical actions. He should apologize to Richards for having the nerve, strength and heart to step to the plate and try to right a wrong to a person not worthy to receive such an important apology.

Still busy and still hustling, Rev. Jackson joined with other "leaders" to "bury" the "N-word". The rapper Nas was once in Rev. Jackson's scope as he protest Nas album concerning the "n-word." After all of the "hustling", Rev. Jackson eventually called Barack Obama a "nigga" in public but didn't mean to be heard and worse than that, he wished for President Obama to be castrated. DAMN! I have been side tracked by Rev. Jackson's hypocrisies so, allow me to pause for a second to rediscover the purpose of this chapter. This chapter is aimed to shine the spotlight on sexually related business or affairs.

Rev. Jackson and his wife have five children but Rev. Jackson has six children. It came out in 2001 that Rev. Jackson had and affair with Karen Stanford. Together they created a baby girl. Rev. Jackson was not the best father to his new baby girl for the first two years. So that's 8 people total that had a situation to look forward to dealing with because of one man, that's not counting other family, friends, media, congregations, churches and the average American citizen something to contemplate about our leaders, churches and future. For a man to leave home at 12;15 am headed to the store to get gas for work in the morning and comes back home at 1:30 with a $100.00 less than he left with; doesn't mean that he don't love his wife or girlfriend and children. However he "blew" his money does not undercut his feelings for his wife and family, "wifey" is safe, he aint going no where. But for a man or woman to go out of there way to prepare and lie to arrange meetings and dates require a lot of dishonesty and degrees of deceptive measures. Having a mistress is a pretty bad thing in some people view but yet that is a personal matter whether it is physical or emotional but to give your mistress at least 35,000 in gifts and money and the promise of at least 40,000 more is a little extra, especially when the money that he was giving was coming from the Rain/Push Organization. What's going on when the youth of America trust rappers more than ministers? What's happening when the youth in America care more about Damon Dash and Jay-Z mending their brother ship than anything that Rev. Jesse Jackson has to say? Rev. Jackson really isn't any worse than anyone else except, it is a shame that he wasn't strong enough not to fall victim to sexual affairs. Children are a blessing and indeed he is blessed with his daughter however, he has really lost the look and respect that he wants or maybe thought that he deserved. Rev. Jesse Jackson probably should continue attending rallies and coming out however, just don't talk but; thanks for everything.

Pastor Ted

Ted Haggard was born in 1956 in Indiana. At the early age of 16, Ted Author Haggard became a born again Christian and went on to attend Oral Roberts University. By 1984, he had become associate pastor of Bethel World Prayer Center in Baton Rouge, Louisiana. Pastor Ted next move was to Colorado Springs, Colorado where he started "New Life Ministries" out of his basement. "Pastor Ted" married Gayle Alcorn in 1978 and would eventually share five children with her. By 2006, "Pastor Ted had been invited into many American homes by way of tell-lie-vision and radio, he was welcomed to visit the White House. "New Life Ministers church" grew to over 13,000 members and resume doing business from a campus in Colorado Springs. "Pastor Ted was head of the National Association of Evangelicals. While leader of NAE, he stated that "homosexual activity, like adulterous relationships, is clearly condemned in the scriptures."

Mike Jones, a masseur and a male prostitute alleged that "Art" "Pastor Ted" paid him for sex almost every month for at least three years. The male prostitute describes the business ship to be strictly physical. He admitted being paid a couple hundred dollars each date and would sometimes be tipped a bit more. Mike agreed to take a polygraph test on a KHOW radio show. The part of the test about having sex with "Pastor Ted" indicated deception. I remember my great grandmother use to say "don't believe nothing that you hear and only half of what you see." "Pastor Ted" first responded by denying to even knowing the male prostitute, and said "I have never had a gay relationship with anybody." On Nov. 3, 2006, "Pastor Ted" admitted to buying methamphetamines and a massage from the male prostitute but claims to not have used the drugs and tossed them in the trash can. New Life church released a statement on Nov. 4, 2006 saying "our investigation and Pastor Haggard's public statements have proven without a doubt that he has committed sexually immoral conduct" "Pastor Ted" was released of his duties. "Pastor Ted" sent a letter of apology to New Life church saying that "I am sorry for the circumstances that has caused me shame and embarrassment for all of you… The fact is that I am guilty of sexual immorality and I take responsibility for the entire problem. I am a deceiver and a liar. There is a part of my life that is so repulsive and dark that I've been warring against it all of my adult life.

The accusations that have been leveled against me are not all true, but enough of them are true that I have been appropriately and lovingly removed from ministry." "Pastor Ted" coming from the school of Oral Roberts definitely leaned how to ask for money and not forfeit and received other benefits from New Life church on the condition that he pack-up and leave Colorado Springs area. He pack-up his wife and severance pay of about 135,000 and moved away. It's reported that he has moved back to Colorado Springs, Co. to open an insurance company. "Pastor Ted" may be a better man and a better person for his past but it's too bad that another one fell victim too his lower desires and lost his life's work.

Coy Privette

Coy Claurance Privette was born in 1933 and grew up to become Rev. Privette, a conservative activist and Baptist minister in North Carolina. Rev. Privette plan to run for Governor of North Carolina as the republican nominee but lost to David Flaterty in the primary however, Rev. Privette did serve in North Carolina House of Representatives and was a minister for at least 12 years as well as a county commissioner. By the end of 2007, Rev. Privette had also became the victim of his lower desires and found him self being charged with aiding and abetting prostitution, the investigation stem from a check from Coy Privette that led to Tiffany Denise Summers. The checks led to warrants that alleged Coy Privette for paying Tiffany Summers (a known and previously convicted prostitute). Why in the hell did he do "business" with a check? "Tricks" have to learn to stay current on how not to get caught tricking, or stop tricking before they lose it all. As a result, Rev. Privette was stripped of his position as county commissioner as well as vice president of programs by the Cabarrus County Men Club in addition to resigning as President of North Carolina's Christian Action League.

Jimmy Swaggert- Jim Bakker- Marvin Gorman

Cons, scams, hypocrisy and paying for sex is not a new thing by any stretch of the imagination. In 1986, "rap battles" and what we know as hip-hop was on the rise but there were other battles going on, on the other side of town. Rev. Jimmy Swaggert waged battle against fellow televangelist Marvin Gorman and Jim Bakker. Apparently, Rev. Swaggert wanted to expose Gorman's affair with a congregational member as well as Rev. Jimmy Bakker's infidelity. By 1988, Rev. Jimmy Swagget had been forced to step down from his pulpit position because of his own business ships with prostitutes and for committing adultery Rev. Swaggert later said that "I have sinned against you, my lord and I would ask that your precious blood would wash and cleanse every stain until it is in the seas of God's forgiveness". Rev. Swagget also had to be delusional to start "beef" against someone else for their sin when he was guilty of basically the same thing. Rev. Jesse Jackson and most of these "con ministers" have a degree of arrogance about them that really shows their simplicity. Sex is indeed a natural thing but just stay out of the pulpits when you are involved with the sex and money business. So many ladies like groupies are fascinated with ministers because ministers is sometimes symbolic to their God and would certainly like to claim and be seen with such a man that reflects God. Some of these ladies don't even consider that the minister is married and still a man until she receives him at a time or moments of weakness, after the realization of the fantasy of promises and future, some of the mistresses become bitter and "turn on" the voluntary affair that she carried out with the minister with hopes of diminishing his credibility and it often works perfectly. A minister really has no room for such an error. Sometimes it seems too easy to be a Christian because some often depend on prayer to make-up for wrong doings. Again, sex is a natural thing and by nature the woman is most certainly a blessing to all creations but just as any other thing of nature; wind, water, fire, anything out of control leads to death of some sort.

Oral Roberts

Oral Roberts has been a household name since I was a young child. As my great grandmother grew older and weaker, she was listed at our local church on the "sick and shut-in" list but she would yet be home looking at Oral Roberts on the mornings that she just couldn't find the strength to get up, get dressed and go to church. My family was the average middle class family that didn't have an abundance of money yet she always paid her tithe at church and supported Oral Roberts Ministry.

Oral Roberts was a televangelist that occasionally revealed his encounter with God. He shared with his audience and tell-lie-vision congregation that God told him, "that if he didn't raise 8 million dollars by a certain time that he would call him home" it was unclear the method that God would use to kill him but during the statement, Rev. Roberts did shed a few tears. As a result of the teary act "con"fession, he received 9.1 million dollars simply by asking for it and his position didn't hurt matters. Rev. Roberts was successful at raising money on different occasions because he was dedicated and mastered his "con"gregation. I really have to give Mr. Rev. Oral Roberts his "props". GOOD ONE!

Joe Barron is in his early fifties and was a minister at Preston Wood Baptist church in Plano Texas and one of the biggest churches in America with at least 26,000 members. Rev. Barron was arrested in 2008 in Dallas Texas for solicitation of a minor on May 15 following an internet sex sting. By May 17, 2008, Pastor Jack Graham was "con"fronting the congregation of Rev. Barron's resignation.

This chapter has list a few male ministers that have been alleged to or proven to be involved in some sort of scam or "scandal" but none of this is new.

There are stories of "sex scandals" and ministers that date back to the 1920's with Aimee Semple McPherson and beyond but, **Aimee Semple McPherson** was a female evangelist, said to have faked her own death to cover an extra marital affair. Her claim for being missing is that she was kidnapped but the kidnapping could never be proved but neither could any wrong doing on her behalf. Females hustle so differently than men; females will think first. The average female will not go to the store at 12:15 a.m. and return at 1:30 a.m. looking and talking crazy. If she meet a guy at the store and have the desire to cheat on her man, she may walk back in the house and say that she forgot that she and a girlfriend have a lunch or dinner appointment coming up the next day or days following it may even be planned for weeks. At the same time, her husband or boyfriend is so clueless that he starts making his own plans and preparing to send his woman into the hand of another man. In case you haven't read about your favorite minister being involved with drama, and "scandal" then, here you go:

- 2008 Rev. Todd Bently

- 2008 Tony Alamo

- 2007 Bishop Earl Paulk

- 2007 Phil Driscoll

- 2007 Richard Roberts

- 2006 Paul Barnes

- 2006 Lonnie Lathem

- 2006 Kent Hovind

- 2004 Rev. Douglas Gordman

- 2000 Rev. John Paulk

- 2000 Rev. Frank Houston

- 1991 Rev. Robert Tilton

- 1991 Rev. Mike Warnke

- 1987 Rev. Peter Popoff

- 1970 Lonnie Frisbee

Aimee Semple McPherson was born Aimee Elizabeth Kennedy in Ontario, Canada. She became Aimee E. Semple after marrying a Pentecostal Missionary name Robert J. Semple in 1908 and by 1910; Robert had died after contracting Malaria during an evangelical tour through Hong Kong. Months after Roberts's death, Aimee gave birth to her and Roberts's daughter "Roberta Star Semple." By 1912, Aimee Semple met Harold Stewart McPherson who soon became her second husband and she became Aimee Semple McPherson. Harold and Aimee became the parents of a baby boy name Rolf Potter Kennedy McPherson. After the birth of her son, Aimee suffered from depression however, by 1913, she was a full time Preacher. Around 1922, Aimee started the Four Square Gospel Church and over saw the construction of Angelus Temple located near the Echo Parks community in Los Angeles, CA. The Temple was built to accommodate at least 5000 seats. Aimee and Harold McPherson were divorced in 1921.

Aimee was known for her soft sex appeal with a mixture of flamboyance which helped increase her congregation. With a larger congregation, Aimee was skillful and tactful at raising money. In the early 20's, Aimee became the first woman in history to preach a radio sermon and in 1924, a Gospel-owned radio station (KFSG), she was the first female to be given a broadcast license by the Federal Communications Commission. Before Aimee Semple McPherson's third marriage to actor David Hutton in 1931, (caused trouble in the church, she preached against marring again while spouse is still alive). In 1926, Aimee and an associate went to Venice Beach for a swim, Aimee suddenly disappeared. On the other side of town; Kenneth G. Ormiston, an employee for the Gospel radio station KFSG, also was missing. There was a massive search for Aimee's body to be recovered a couple of people died during the rescue, and sea side vigils were carried out. The tragedy was covered by radio and newspapers. On June 23, 32 days after Aimee's disappearance, she strutted off a Mexican dessert near Douglas Arizona. She claims to have been drugged with chloroform, kidnapped and tortured. To escape, she alleged walked 13 hours to safety.

Aimee told her kidnapping story while being fully dressed but she only had on a swim suite at the time of her disappearance, she even had on a watch given to her by her mother that she didn't take on the swimming trip. There was no evidence to support Aimee's kidnapping, torture story and when she would not clear up the story about her relationship with Kenneth Ormiston, Judge Sammuel Blake charged her with obstruction of Justice Nov. 3. January 10, 1927, district attorney Asa Keys dropped all charges because of lack of evidence. Aimee Semple McPherson and Harold Hutton divorced in 1934, in 1944, Aimee was found dead from an overdose of barbiturates. The Four Square Gospel Church is still in operation with over 2 million member congregation, with her son Rolf Potter Kennedy McPherson in leadership position.

Ministers, Preachers, Evangelist etc. should not take for granted that Jesus died for his sins and claim his own sins. The pulpit is not a play pen every word that is spoken in the pulpit should be believed and lived by the person speaking it. When speaking from the pulpit, a person should be able to put his life on each word that he speaks. Preachers that fall victim to their lower desires are looked at worse, in many cases; church is some people last hope. The appearances of a con or scam from Preachers are often devastating.

Mark 10:19
- Thou knowest the commandments, do not commit adultery, do not kill, do not steal, Do not bear false witness, Defraud not, Honor thy father and mother.

Mark 10:11-12
- 11. And he saith unto them, whosever shall put away his wife, and marry another, committeth adultery against her.

- 12. And if a woman shall put away her husband, and be married to another, committeth adultery.

Deut. 17:17
- Neither shall he multiply wives to himself that his heart turns not away: neither shall he greatly multiple to himself silver and gold.

IF
"If you can keep your head when all about you
Are losing theirs and blaming it on you,
If you can trust yourself when all men doubt You
But make allowance for their doubting too,
If you can wait and not be tired by waiting,
Or being lied about, don't deal in lies,
Or being hated, don't give way to hating,
And yet don't look too good, nor talk too wise:

If you can dream—and not make dreams your Master,
If you can think—and not make thoughts your Aim;
If you can meet with Triumph and Disaster
And treat those two impostors just the same;
If you can bear to hear the truth you've spoken
Twisted by knaves to make a trap for fools,
Or watch the things you gave your life to, Broken,
And stoop and build'em up with worn-out Tools:

If you can make one heap of all your winnings

And risk it all on one turn of pitch-and-toss,
And lose, and start again at your beginnings'
and never breath a word about your loss;
If you can force your heart and nerve and Sinew
To serve your turn long after they are gone,
And so hold on when there is nothing in you
Except the Will which says to them: "Hold On!"

If you can talk with crowds and keep your Virtue,
Or walk with kings—nor lose the common Touch,
If neither foes nor loving friends can hurt you;
If all men count with you, but none too much,
If you can fill the unforgiving minute
With sixty seconds' worth of distance run,
Yours is the Earth and everything that's in it,
And—which is more—you'll be a Man, my son!"

--Rudyard Kipling

Chapter 2

The Power of Politicians
Unseen
Spending
Savagely
WHY

Political sex scandals are nothing new, they go back to **Thomas Jefferson**, who had sex with his slaves. Years ago, politicians seem to survive scandals a little more successfully. **Grover Cleveland** was also chastised for having an illegitimate child. Who could forget Senator **Strom Thurmond** from South Carolina? During the early and mid part of Senator Thurmond's career, it would be no surprise to hear him advocating separation among the races. In the early 1900's, it was common for an older man to marry a younger women. Strom Thurmond did not marry his young lover (Carrie "Tunch" Butler) who was a 16 year old black girl, as well as the family maid. Thurmond was 22 at the time. Carrie "Tunch" Butler gave birth to Strom Thurmond's daughter October 12, 1925. Age was not a major issue in the early 1900s but Thurmond lost the respect of some peers because of his hypocrisy which was caused by him not being strong enough to reframe from sex with a black woman and not having the courage to publicly admit it.

Some people find amusement when the spotlight is on a political scandal. A politician does not have to only be caught with a business woman to lose his job, reputation, family, finances and career. A married politician that has an affair is treated like a criminal in the media. Some extra marital affairs are genuine love ships and punishment seems to be cruel and usual.

(Senator and U.S. Presidential Candidate) **Gary Hart** was found out to be cruising together on a yacht named "Monkey Business" with a young, pretty, sexy "business woman" named Donna Rice. As a result of the "Monkey Business", Gary Hart lost a real chance of becoming President of the United States of America.

(Political Strategist) **Dick Morris** was known and is still known for being a brilliant man yet, he too has been the victim in what some may call a victimless crime. Morris was caught in an expensive Washington Hotel with a "business woman". Morris was said to impress the woman by calling and having a conversation with a very important person (Most likely to gain more acceptance). The person Morris happened to call in the Presence of the business woman was former President Bill Clinton. These events happened in 1994, by 1996; Morrison was released from the re-election campaign but not before receiving a reputation from enjoying toe sucking. Damn! Some women talk too much.

(U.S. Congressman: Presidential Candidate) **Wilbur Mills** was an Arkansas democrat. Mills was pulled over by the police on a routine traffic stop. During the traffic stop, mills was found to be intoxicated and in the company of a stripper (business woman) named Fannie Fox. Once the police pulled over Mills, Fannie Fox leaped from the car and ran. Mills often frequented the strip club where his favorite business woman worked. The scandal was not easily overlooked and forgotten. As a result of Wilbur Mills being in love with a stripper, he checked himself into a hospital and said that he was a "sick man"

(Senator R- Louisiana) **David Vitter** was the Dennis Rodman of politics. Vitter was first connected to Deborah Jean Palfrey the "DC Madam" and soon after he was linked to Jeanette Maier; a New Orleans Madam and a business woman that worked in her brothel that goes by the name Wendy Ellis Cortez. Vitter admitted to being involved with "DC Madam" but he didn't hurriedly admit to the New Orleans prostitute. Wendy Cortez and Jeanette Maier admitted that Vitter was a client of the Canal Street Brothel. Maier said that she first met Vitter at a fishing rodeo where she and her "business women" were hired to entertain politicians. Maier went on to leak that Vitter was a "decent guy" that may have only needed company. "He's not a freak, he's not using drugs, and he's not using tax payers' money to buy hookers or drugs or anything like that. **He's just a decent, normal guy**" she said. Vitter was elected and has until 2010 to convince voters that he only wants to sleep with one woman for the rest of his life no matter how boring or predictable it may become.

(U.S. congressman D-Massachusetts) **Barney Frank** was reprimanded by the House once it was learned that his male partner ran an escort service out of Frank's home.

(Maryland House of Delegates) **Charles Boutin** was Maryland's Public Service Commissioner. Boutin resigned after being reported of soliciting prostitutes on-line while still serving in the legislature.

Even **Arnold Schwarzenegger (R-CA)** had to admit to inappropriate conduct with a woman when he was an actor and professional body builder. It is hard to understand the thrill of making politicians admit to having sex. Are politicians that have a lot of sex partners less patriotic? We all probably know a smart man with lots of sex partners that could possible be a great politician. Whenever the word scandal is used, it mostly involves a politician or authority figure. A scandal is nothing more than what the public or press decides it to be. Sometimes the media feeds the publics desires regardless of the truth.

A man would agree that if he could have sex anytime with anyone that he wanted to, he believes that he would be a happier man. Some men view sex as the greatest meal he's ever had but is hungry soon after. There are many genetic impulses we must control for the sake of civilization, but it's a little much when a man's entire career, family, and life can and has been destroyed because of one weakness, one woman.

The following is a list of politicians that have been involved with or mention in connection to sexual related scandals. These politicians are not all guilty and not all innocent of the allegations made against them. The list is quite long and some would say pointless, but it does illustrate how many men fall victim to their lower desires and start to neglect business. With certain positions, innocent means nothing; men are often judged and pre-judged through associations. Hopefully, men will learn from mistakes of the elders and realize that sagging jeans and white shirts are not a separation of who they are as people. Sometimes the misfortunes of some inspire others. Young men of Urban America are now realizing that a politician is a regular man, with average faults just like him. Some men used to believe that they could not achieve certain goals because they didn't come from the "right" background, family or wasn't perfect. Now the business is being smart, alert, and attentive to business. No matter what is said, the American public and politicians have made America a great country.

From **2000-2009** there were approximately 32 political scandals, involving:

- Jeff Gannon

- Larry Craig (R-D)

- Eliot Spitzer

- Paul J. Morrison (D-KS)

- Arnold Schwarzenegger (R-CA)

- Randall L. Tobias (R)

- Vito Fossella (R-NY)

- Kevin Shealy (D-CA)

- John Edwards (D-NC)

- Jack Ryan (R-IL)

- Gary Condit (D-CA)

- Don Sherwood (R-PA)

- Bob Allen (R-FL)

- John Burton (D-CA)

- Mark Foley (R-FL)

- Jim West (R)

- Jim McGreevy

- Steven C. LaTourette (R-OH)

- Bob Wise (D-W)

- Paul Patton (D-KY)

- Marc Dann (D-OH)

- Ed Schrock (R-VA)

- Gavin Newsom (D-CA)

- Roosevelt Dobbins (D-AR)

- The WASHINGTONIENNE Scandal

- Antonio Villaraigosa (D-CA)

- Bob Allen (R-FL)

- Richard Curtis (R-WA)

- Kwame Kilpatrick

- Tim Mahoney (D-FL)

- Glen Murphy Jr. (R)

- David Vitter (R-LA)

1990-1999 Approximately 7 scandals involving:

- Former President Bill Clinton (D-AR)

- Clarence Thomas (R)

- Ken Calvert (R-CA)

- Bob Bar (R-GA)

- Arlan Stangeland (R-MN)

- Mel Reynolds (D-IL)

- Chuck Robb (D-VA)

1980-1989 Approximately 14 scandals involving:

- Donald "Buz" Lukens (R-OH)

- John Hinson (R-MS)

- Paul Ingram (R-WA)

- Gerry Studds (D-MA)

- Gus Savage (D-IL)

- Thomas Evans (R-DE)

- Jim Bates (D-CA)

- Richard Garner

- Gary Hart (D-CO)

- Brock Adams (D-WA)

- Barney Frank (D-MA)

- Robert Bauman (R-MD)

- Ernie Konnyu (R-CA)

- John Schmitz (R-CA)

1970-1979 Approximately 6 political sex scandals:
- Fred Richmond (D-NY)

- Wilbur Mills (D-AR)

- John Young (D-TX)

- Neil Goldschmidt (D-OR)

- Allen Howe (D-UT)

- Wayne Hayes (D-OH)

1900-1969 8 political sex scandals

- President Warren Harding (R)

- Eugene Schmitz

- Newport Sex Scandal

- Strom Thurmond

- President James Buchanan

- Petticoat or Eaton Affairs

- Walter Jenkins

- Alexander Hamilton

President **Thomas Jefferson** was the 3rd president of the United States and the father of the Declaration of Independence. He fathered a child with Sally Hemings, his 17 year old slave.

Whether a person is guilty or innocent of a crime or scandal, it is always good to be on the defensive side of business in order to keep a good name, good reputation; do good business, avoid trouble and scandal.

In the 1960s, when opponents viewed one another as a threat; then many times assassination was the solution. The new weapon today is Character assassination. Politicians are being destroyed without a fire being shot. Detectives, former CIA and FBI operatives, intelligence and security agencies are hired to dig up politicians' sex lives, etc… Some politicians are known to hire damage control experts. The "fixer" usually cleans up the mess before it becomes news or a scandal. Many times the cases that a fixer is involved with could be: adultery, bribery, abortion, sex tapes, deviate sexual behavior, bi-sexuality, homo sexuality or blackmail. The "fixer" negotiates with political enemies of his client. In many cases, the mistress or male lover is usually paid off in cash or a car. Political enemies are sometimes promised votes on certain bills. Some fixers receive $50,000-$100,000 even before they agree to take the case.

A Fixer is hired to clean up a person's mess, to repair their reputation. Do you remember? **Vernon Jordan, Don Crutchfield or Anthony Pellicano**

- Vernon Jordan was a fixer for President Bill Clinton

- Don Crutchfield worked for Donald and Marla Trump, Lisa Marie Presley, O.J. Simpson, Tim Allen and Carroll O'Connor

- Anthony Pellicano was a fixer for Michael Jackson, Sylvester Stallone, Roseanne, and Kevin Costner.

It seemed to make good business for every man with money or dreams of having money to make wise decisions or be ready to hire a fixer. For the men that can't afford a "fixer", you should put in an application to be a "fixer"; it seems they get paid good money. There is still a list of politicians involved in sexual related cases.

Brock Adams (U.S. Senator) did not seek re-election after being accused by eight women of sexual harassment, rape and sexual assault.

Wayne Hayes (U.S. Congressman) was forced to resign. He showed trick tendencies when he put his mistress on the pay roll. He had been in congress for 28 years.

Bob Livingston (U.S. Congressman) seems to be on his way to becoming speaker of the house before reportedly having an extra marital affair and resigning from congress

James McGreevy (former Gov. of N.J) admitted to having an affair with his homeland security advisor and resigned as governor.

Don Sherwood (U.S. Congressman) lost his safe house seat after reports of an extra marital affair.

Rudy Giluliani (former Mayor of N.Y) 2008 run for the white house caught unwanted attention concerning his current wife who he was said to be cheating on his ex-wife with. Some people believe that story hurt Giluliani's chances for the White House.

Kwame Kilpatrick (D-MI) Former Detroit Mayor has lost tremendously because of reasons involving an extramarital affair with his chief-of-staff, Christine

Beaty. "Inappropriate" text messages were discovered between the two. Kilpatrick is also said to be linked to a woman in North Carolina name Carmen Slowsky.

THE RESULTS OF A SCANDAL

Married men and single men alike have taken a beat down once being linked to business women. MEN HAVE SUFFERED under the terms dog, two-timer, cheater, adulterer, even criminal given the circumstances. While at the same time they are getting divorces because of these matters, some may go on to marry the (gold-digger) business woman; get divorced and sued by the same lady for half his earnings, black mailed, being fired, humiliated and forced to resign from his job or position. Some are depositing babies into these females and some are even going to jail. In some cases, to avoid a jail sentence, a "Trick" may have the option to pay $250.00 to attend a sex offender course for 4-7hours a session called "John School" (true story). After "John School" the misdemeanor charges of solicitation of a prostitute are dropped as long as the "John" is not caught again within the next 6 months. Schools are located in 6 major cities: Washington, New York City, San Francisco, Pittsburgh, West Palm Beach, and Buffalo N.Y.

Artist: Jay-Z & R. Kelly f/ Devin the Dude
Album: The Best of Both Worlds
Song: Pussy

"[Devin the Dude]
Pussy is a whole different aspect of life
Wars don' started from country to country, over they women
Pussy, is one of the most powerful thangs in the world
And a lot of people don't understand how powerful pussy is
Pussy make "n"s, blow they brains out, they bitch brains out
Uh, uh, pussy make people do thangs they never would think they'd do

[Chorus: Jay-Z]
The power of the p-u-s-s-y
That's why every "m***********" in the world dress fly
Every baller that can afford it, they cop the best ride
For the power of the p-u-s-s-y, let's have some fun
S-s-y, that's why "n"s get they hair cuts, try to dress fly
Every baller that can afford it, he cop the best ride
For the power of the p-u-s-s-y

[Jay-Z]
I know this girl we call her Sweet Cooch Brown
Hands down, mami had the bombest pussy in town
One dip in the girl pool, that's all it took
One sample of the snapple, and ya ass was whupped
Have you buyin' Gucci sandals, matchin' pocket books
Blowin' up her beeper ringin' her phone off the hook
Bll players they spit money, rappers they spit time
All a while they both clamin' that they never spent a dime
Business guys, she would victimize
Have 'em paying rent on condos in the Miami high rise
We ask her, who pussy is this look her right in her eyes
She said this pussy's yours daddy, tell 'em nothin' but lies
They didn't believe it, but they wanted to, needed to
She had the type of body, that you didn't want leavin' you
So they ignored all her flirtin' ways
And put a ring on her finger I'm like, Earth to Dave

[Chorus: Jay-Z]
The power of the p-u-s-s-y
That's why every motherfucker in the world dress fly
Every baller that can afford it, that gotta have the best ride
The power of the p-u-s-s-y
The power of the p-u-s-s-y
That's why "n"s get they hair cuts, try to dress fly
Every baller that can afford it, they cop the best ride
For the power of the p-u, I see you

[R. Kelly]
I ain't no rapper, but I'ma say my shit
When it comes down to that "m***********" clit, clit, clit
"N"s are sick, sick, sick, turn on you quick, quick, quick
That's why I be givin' mami much, dick, dick, dick
Why chumps be coppin' them furs, and all that
Feining for this pussy, as if y'all was on crack
When it comes to the truth, I can't hold back
Y'all cats that be babysittin', and these broads need to be smacked
It's this "n" named Monroe, that I know from way back
He hit the lotto bought his girl a Cadillac
Now this bitch be creepin' behind this "n"s back
He busted her guess what, he still took the bitch back
3 things "n"s love, money, pussy, and drugs
Can't get one without the other 'less you soft and in love
Now take it from a player whose done all the above
"N"s it's the lesbian, R&B thug

[Chorus: Jay-Z]
The power of the p-u-s-s-y
That's why every motherfucker in the world dress fly
Every baller that can afford it, that gotta have the best ride
The power of the p-u-s-s-y
The power of the p-u-s-s-y
That's why "n"s get they hair cuts, try to dress fly
Every baller that can afford it, they cop the best ride
For the power of the p-u, I see you

[R. Kelly]
"N"s would do anything
For some pussy, hey, hey, hey, oh
See it don't matter who you are
Where ya from, in this life
At some point, you're gonna wanna
Get you some, yes you will, oooo, uuuh"

Chapter 3

FOUL PLAYS

- Warren G. Harding

- Standford White

- Alexander Hamilton

- Silvio J. Failla

- Author Brown

- Bill Mahr

- Bill O'Reilly

- Burt Reynolds

- Glenn Rice

- Patrick Roy

- Ronnie Belliard

- Alex Rodriguez

- Damon Dash

- Joe Buddens

- Aaron Hall

- Rae Curruth

Today in America, women are fighting for the rights to be treated equal to men. A lot of women are just as aggressive as the man in the work place and business world. This is a lost for men. Some times women say and do things that a man deserves to get punched out for. To punch a man is more respectful to him than an open hand slap. The open hand slap was intended to be used on a female but, now-a-days, females are even complaining about that. It's not suggested to hit a female in any shape, form or fashion simply because, it is ugly for business. It's hard to make and save money from behind bars and retaining attorneys. Being in jail works against any hustle, job, business, scam, etc. it's very important not to break the law when your goal is too build capital. "Get Money"!

Sometimes it seems that the only defense that a man has to stay free and have money is to be humble. Instead of getting angry enough at a female to hurt or kill her, he some times have to put him self on time-out and evaluate the situation, or just count his loses and walk away but, understanding the risk of lost from the start. If the "trick" potential husband divorces her then half of his money may possibly go to her. Why? He made the money why can't he keep it?

For instance Glenn Rice is a former NBA player for the Miami Heats. Rice just so happen to find his wife hiding Alberto Perez in the closet. After taking a beating from Rice, Alberto Perez called the police. Rice had his wife living in one of America more exclusive neighbor hoods in America. Glenn Rice worked hard his entire career, married Christina Fernandez Rice to love and share with. He was arrested and charged with assault and battery after she invited another man into the home. Rice was released on $5000.00 bond which was the beginning; the trouble had only just begun on Jan. 11, 2008.

Patrick Roy

Patrick Roy is known for being goalie in the NHL. Roy was arrested on domestic violence charges after the police witness the scene of him and his wife's resident after a hang-up 911 call. After the investigation, Roy was cleared of charges yet there is no winning to such allegations. Roy was cleared partly because the damaged that he caused to the property belong to him, the prosecutors wanted to argue that it belongs to his wife as well even though he paid for it. If he should be in jail and leave her in his house. WHY EVEN GET MARRIED IF IT IS POSSIBLE TO GO TO JAIL for getting up-set and destroying your own property?

Alexander Hamilton

In 1791, President Alexander Hamilton had a two year affair with Maria Renolds only to find out he had been conned by her and her husband, Hamilton was blackmailed for over $1000 which was a lot of money in 1791. That eventually had an influence on his political authority and suggestions.

Warren G. Harding

President Warren G. Harding found him self in a similar situation as Alexander Hamilton. Harding had an affair with Carrie Phillips and was said to have paid her $20,000 to keep quiet about the affair. Harding also said to had an affair with Nan Britton, a woman 30 years younger that he made a deposit of a $baby girl$. It was learned that he probably had sex with her in every room and closet in the White House.

Gary Dourdan

Gary Dourdan plays an investigator on the hit T.V. show C.S.I. Dourdan was accused of rape by his ex-lover (Anne Greene). Although Dourdan entered a plea of no contest to the misdemeanor battery and was sentenced to stay away from the alleged victim and attend domestic violence counseling. Dourdan later filed a lawsuit against the accuser for 4 million dollars for slander and infliction of emotional distress. Dourdan claimed that Greene is a "fatal attraction"

THE BUSINESS OF PROPER THOUGHT:

The sequence of chance events could be devastating concerning the sex business.

(NFL football Player) Warren Moon was sued by Michelle Eaves, a former Vikings cheerleader, and also a former exotic dancer. She claimed that Moon made unwanted sexual advances; she **con**sulted with her husband about avoiding "Moon". She accused Moon of insisting on oral sex after she arrived at his hotel room. Even though Moon denied charges, the case was settled for $150,000.

Michael Jordan

Michael Jordan sued Karla Knafel for attempting to extort 5 million dollars from him to keep their affair secret. Jordan and Knafel both admitted to the three year affair.

Alex Rodriguez decided to have a little fun in 2004 and partied with a stripper a couple of times. He probably chose the stripper by her visual appeal and how sorry he felt for her. A lot of tricks really have intentions on helping these girls but, this one particular stripper (Candice Houlihan, 31) cheered on Rodriguez wife to get tons of cash after divorce. Candice Houlihan appeared to be more of a groupie than a "business woman".

Ronnie Belliard is known for playing second base for the St. Louis Cardinals, Belliard had a one night stand with the daughter of George Edwards. After learning of this, Edwards reached out to extort Belliard for $150,000. Knowing that Belliard was married, the odds were good until after he received the first payment of $25,000 and said that his daughter had a miscarriage but still attempted to demand the remaining $125,000 to keep quiet about the one night stand. George Edwards and his daughter could also be considered "groupies".

Bill O'Reilly was somehow forced to file claims of extortion, infliction of emotional distress and wrongful interference with contractual relations. According to the complaint filed by Fox News Network, LLC; and William O'Reilly against Andrea Mackris, Benedict P. Morrell: and Benedict P. Morrell & Associates P.C.

Nature of the Action

"This action responds to defendant's extortion scheme. Defendants seek to extort sixty million dollars ($60 million) from plaintiffs in return for not going public with a scandalous and scurrilous claim based on alleged inappropriate comments made to Mackris by O'Reilly. Defendant's outrageous demand cannot be justified by any alleged harm that Mackris claims to have suffered. Rather, Defendants demand is based on their threat to sully the reputations of a successful cable news network and a nationally renowned television and radio hose, columnist, and author. Their demand is black mail, Pure and Simple". This is HOW TO HANDLE BUSINESS, IT IS NEVER RECOMMENDED to learn the ways of Rae Curruth. Michael Jordan, and Bill O'Reilly both played fair and they played to win.

Burt Renolds eventually filed extortion charges against his ex-girlfriend. Pamela M. Seals accused Renolds of yelling at her and stomping her toes. Seals were offered a million dollars but she didn't agree. She must felt like ex-girlfriends of rich guys deserve more for a toe stomping.

Bill Maher seems to like the extremely finest "business women". One of his ex-girlfriends Nancy Johnson a.k.a Coco is also a model, she filed a $9 million palimony suite against him claiming that he subjected her to physical and verbal abuse, including humiliating and insulting her. Johnson and Mahr dated 17 months he supposedly made promises for millions of dollars. If she believed him then she has to be demoted to a bootlegger for "buying dreams". Coco complaints included:

1. Breach of contract

2. Promissory Estoppels

3. Promissory Fraud

4. Battery

5. Assault   Coco wanted 9 million dollars

(Rapper) **Earl Simmons** ("DMX") was accused of sodomy sexual abuse and false imprisonment by a stripper that was 29 at the time, left the strip club to go stay the rest of the night with him.

(Rapper) **Calvin Broadus** "Snoop Dog" was accused by Kyle Bell, a make-up artist of drugging and raping her along with four other men. Bell sought to sue "snoop for 25 million dollars". Kyle Bell did not report the alleged rape to the police until four months afterwards. Snoop eventually file a pre-emptive law suit claiming to be the target of extortion.

(Producer) **Damon Dash** was accused by a model name Kristie Thompson of raping her for 10-15 seconds while allegedly she was high on ecstasy and champagne. It seems that a female, "business woman" at any state of mind can and will have an affect on the welfare of a man. If Thompson believes her hallucinations, and believes she deserves 8-15 million dollars for 10-15 seconds of drunken sex, and then something is seriously wrong.

Stanford White was born in 1853, Stanford grew to be a well-known architect and was assistant to Henry Hobson Richardson, one of the greatest architects of their times and of American History. White went on to design the second of four **Madison Square Gardens,** which Whites design opened in 1890. Whites designs included: First Bowery Savings Bank in 1894, Judson Memorial Church, Washington Square Arch in 1889, The Cable building, Madison Square Presbyterian Church, New York Herald Building and the Century Building all located in New York City. Through-out White's career, he was known for his "shingle style designs, as well as Fifth Avenue mansions for families such as the Vander bitts and the Astors.

White was also known for being a ladies man and was known to take show girls (young chorines) to his bachelor decorated apartment inside Madison Square Garden when it was known as the Giralda Towers. White took a special interest in a particular show girl name Evelyn Nesbit. Over the course of knowing and dating Evelyn, she became involved with a millionaire name Harry K. Thaw. Thaw was an insanely jealous man. Evelyn and Thaw went on to marry. After Thaw found out that Stanford White and Evelyn Nesbit had sex in the past he could never let go of the idea, one night while Nesbit and Thaw went to the Madison Square Garden to attend a show, Thaw, expecting Stanford White to be in attendance, dressed in a big coat covering a gun until he reached White and shot him three times in the face killing him.

Before the trial, Harry Thaws mother reached and agreement with Evelyn Nesbit, to pay her 1 million dollars to testify that her husband was insane so that he may avoid prison, in hopes of receiving the million dollars, Evelyn Nesbit performance on the witness stand deserved and applause. She said that Harry Thaw was protecting her from the abusive Stanford White. Once the trial was over, one of Evelyn lovers was in the grave yard and the other one was sent to an insane asylum. Evelyn Nesbit never received the 1 million dollars.

(New Jersey State Assemblyman) Silvio J. Failla, by age 62, Failla had been to law school, studied to be a pharmacist, he was a funeral director, and a month and two weeks as Mayor of Hoboken. In 1972, Failla met a prostitute name Deborah Bell at a bar in New Jersey. Silvio allegedly proposition a business offer to Deborah Bell. Bell agenda ultimately included her and Theophus King Webster (her pimp) robbing and killing the first term assembly man, in which they succeeded. Witnesses say that Failla last words were "HELP ME"!

Rae Carruth

(NFL Player, Carolina Panthers) Rae Carruth was born Jan 1974, in Sacramento, California; Rae was one of his mothers' two children. His mother was a social worker and basically raised her children alone. After high school, Rae was recruited by the University of Colorado and in 1997; he was the first round draft pick for the Carolina Panthers. Contract was 3.7 million for 4 years. According to friends and co-workers, Rae met a young "business woman" named Cherica Adams at a Strip Club. Cherica had been known to mingle and enjoy the company of Professional athletes. She even worked for the Carolina Panthers for free when accepting to work as an intern during high school. Cherica and Rae shared a friendship for over a year however; Rae shared similar friendships with other females. Cherica announces that she was pregnant and the joy of it was obvious. As a result of Adams becoming pregnant by Rae Carruth; he solicited a couple of acquaintances to assist him in killing Cherica Adams. It worked, Cherica was shot 10 weeks prior to the babies due date and died as a result of the gun shots.

Following the investigation, Rae Carruth was wanted for questioning and possibly a suspect which led to Carruth fleeing to Wildersville, Tenn. and folding his large body into the trunk of a Toyota Camry with bottles to urinate in and snacks as survival food. This is a tragic story even without mentioning the financial loses and obligations of Rae Carruth. This is the aftermath of "BAD BUSINESS".

Senator Arthur Brown

During the late 1800's and early 1900's, Salt Lake City Utah had a resident and a Senator name Arthur Brown. Senator Brown was killed by his mistress who is known to be Mrs. Anna Bradley. While Senator Brown was cold and dead, newspaper articles still had headlines that favored Senator Brown's more negative side yet, he must remain the victim because, he couldn't defend him self, nor his life's work and reputation from the dead. Some of the headlines would have lead you to believe that he deserved to have been killed.

WHAT TO DO WHEN YOU DON'T KNOW WHAT TO DO?

Situation: Young married couple with two children, a boy and a girl. The wife is a nurse's aid and the husband is a drug dealer with a serious and deadly reputation for "Getting money" and taking care of home. He has three brothers that work for him. They all have $350,000 homes in the suburbs. The husband "Mike" is at home with his wife and family one night. After dinner and T.V. they work together to get the children to bed. Mike and his wife go to bed and Mike begins to kiss and caress his wife's body. After a while of pleasure and foreplay, Mike begins to penetrate his wife. After only a little while of making love, Mike's wife vagina is super moist. He slipped out of her, using his hand to place himself back inside his wife, he felt something slippery. After a glance, he noticed; it was a condom, which he and his wife never use. It's from another guy that she had sex with and it slipped off inside of her. Well Mike beat the shit out of her. She ended up calling the cops and telling where the drug stash, money etc. was at. Mike and all of his brothers lost everything and are now serving 25 year sentence's behind her allegations. To save herself-she was responsible for 4 young men leaving their children and family because she's a (cheater) bootlegger.

Situation: David is a 27 year old 6'2 light brown skin dude with a promising future, David was the supervisor at his industrial job, often scheduled to work late nights usually until morning shifts. His girlfriend is 25 years old and work at the same plant but at different hours in a different department. It was rumored that David's girlfriend was having an affair with a guy that also worked at the same plant. One Thursday night, after being at work for a couple hours, his cell phone rang, it was his mother informing him there was an unfamiliar car at his house. Without signing out from the job, David immediately went to the parking area, got in his car, and headed home. David found his girlfriend in their bed with another man. He shot and killed them both and went back to work. He is now serving two life sentence's plus 60 years. How should his mother feel? Sometimes things may be better left unsaid. In many cases, people's love for each other becomes the instrument to their own destruction. We have situation after situation where good guys are going to jail behind the faults and actions of their women playing "the game".

Kevin met Massina and she let him know from day one that she has a man, and if she decides that she wants to "kick it" with him, he can't be "tripping" and that her man comes first. She in fact had a little saying: "I have two rules; 1.) When you ride in the car with me, wear your seat belt. 2.) Don't fall in love! So he didn't. Just so happen, she said all of that before she started to like Kevin more than she ever imagined. That was before she bought him a motorcycle or gave him 8,500 cash. Once she saw him with another girl, it was a different story. As a result, an argument between the two of them reached a climax. She yelled. "f*** it- we will both die", while mashing the gas. As the car reached about 90 mph in a residential neighbor-hood, she turned the wheel making the car flip over multiple times. Neither was injured, Kevin climbed out the car, limped to the other side and beat the shit out of Massina because all he could think was, "I have children, she has a man and she's trying to take me away from my kids. She doesn't have the right." Witness seen Kevin beat Massina after the car crash and Kevin was charged with assault and battery.

There are some scholars, philosophers, teachers and preachers that insist that women are good by nature and were sentence with the responsibility of being mans help-mate. But just as all things of nature; (wind, water, fire) when it is out of control, it leads to death. A woman is no different, and it is wise to understand that death isn't always physical.

Chapter 4

American Divas
(Business Women)

Modern day "Gold diggers" are so ill informed; men are learning that they don't have to be married to have lots of fun with sexy women and even more than one at the same time. Modern day gold diggers are equivalent to most of the teenage drug dealers; they are, doing more for less, and often tell on themselves, their connections and their clients or customers. Some of the modern day "wanna be" business women has done nothing more than look, pretty, tell lies, have sex, notice themselves getting old and apply for a reality show called Atlanta House wives and is known by Sheree or Kim or, a former stripper/model and have sex with lots of men which none of them chose to marry her, she panics or gets mad and start writing books saying that she has attempted to commit suicide, conned and lied to a gang of men to trust that her sex was as good as it looked. (Note to former President George W. Bush), "First time shame on you, second time shame on me". Men, don't be fooled 3 times. She will tell, **Don't Do It!**

Real Business Women should become familiar with real gold diggers and divas of yesterday and today. "The Game is Over"

THIS IS THE BUSINESS!

To my dismay, a lot of females that are getting credit for being Gold diggers and Divas actually are just getting lucky. Picture Anna Nichole planning to deceive (initially). She was simple. After attending a speech given by Author and Professor Julian Shabazz, he spoke on the KISS AFFECT. Keep It Simple Stupid. It's just that simple if a person isn't that smart. Keep it simple, it attracts sympathy and urgency to care for. Attention in return, = business=money.

Babe Paley

Babe Paley was born Barbara Cushing before dying in 1978 at 63 years old as Barbara Cushing Mortimer Paley. "Babe" dad was an internationally known brain surgeon which made financial life for her mother a good one. Experiencing the good life, she taught her three daughters; Barbara, Betsey and Mary Cushing, to hunt down men with not riches but wealth and power. Mary grew up to marry Vincent Asctor and James Fosburgh. Once her divorce to Fosburgh was final, she introduced him to her friend, Brooke Marshall as promised. She understood that her ex-husband needed companionship and they married. Betsey later married James Roosevelt and pro-duced two kids. Yea, that's right, President Franklin D. Roosevelt son.

"Babe" didn't take the risk of shooting for the pros. before finishing college. She attended and graduated from the Winsor school. After landing an ideal job at Vogue, she was now qualified to wheel and deal and she did just that. In 1940 she married a man name Stanley Mortimer, Jr. By 1945 and 1946, she was rich and on the best-dressed list of who's who. Hope you understand there is no "GAME" this is serious business, although by the end of 1946, she was well into her divorce but with two $$children out of the deal and a nice financial settlement. When all she did was; what her mother taught her; to find a man with money. It's just as easy to fraud a rich man as it is a poor man; Modern day Gold diggers are getting pregnant without doing their homework; getting pregnant by men who can't afford the three he has and she didn't even know about, but not "Babe". In 1947, Babe was married to William S. Paley, the founder of CBS and ridiculously wealthy. He wasn't that popular in some social circles but with "Babe", he could be. Her agenda was the security of wealth which made for a win-win marriage and two more $$children$$. That part of the deal may be considered good business. However, her husband was wealthy and other mothers had taught their daughters the same thing which made William Paley become the victim because of his extra marital sexual affairs. However, "Babe Paley" was a beautiful respected icon, educated business woman and truly a Diva, she got back some of the best out of life as she put into it. How could William Paley be a good man and committed husband when daughters are taught to hunt down such a man?

Slim Keith "Slim" Lady Keith

Born Mary Raye Gross in 1916, her mother changed her name to Nancy Gross by the time she had appeared on the cover of Harper's Bazaar at the age of 22. She may be best known with her friend "Babe Paley" as the motivation behind the novel "Answered Prayers". Some divas sing their way into wealth, some are intelligent, educated business women and some marry into it. Nancy was; smart funny, fashionable, and beautiful, often made the best-dressed list, and was the first civilian (private citizen) to receive a Niemen Marcus Fashion Award as well as The "CALIFORNIA GIRL". As the CALIFORNIA GIRL, she was pursued by the likes of Ernest Hemingway, Carey Grant, Clark Gable and Gary Cooper. Nancy was not a groupie and she didn't have to settle, she persuaded Howard Leland Haywood Hawks a film director to divorce his wife of years to pursue her. By 1941, Nancy and Hawks were married and he was building her a mansion in Bel-air. She was beautiful and he was a wealthy victim falling prey to being haunted. The marriage ended but not before she received the deposit of a $baby$. Before Hawks and Nancy could marry, he had to divorce his wife. The same thing happens to "Slim". While on a trip to Spain, her husband, Leland "Hawk" Howard, became friends with Pamela Churchill and, when it was all said and done, she was "Pamela Churchill Hayward". "Keeping it moving"; "Slim" met and married a British millionaire business man, Sir Keith. They didn't love each other, she didn't need his money, they just both had respect for the "business" she could improve his social connections and he could serve as her arm piece, a merger, with no love. They got married and of course it didn't last without any emotional compassion or commitment. "Lady Keith", "Slim Keith" and Sir Keith were headed for divorce. She decided that she could no longer be married to a man that is so obsessed with money. He proposed to have a Mexican divorce to get into a lower tax bracket but she refused and had the divorce in New York City. Slim Keith definitely gets her diva endorsement.

Doris Duke

Doris Duke died in 1993 at 81 years old; she was born the only child to a tobacco and electric energy millionaire. The millions her father had in the early 1900's would equal about a billion U.S. dollars now. Doris learned legalities at an early age when she successfully won against her mother in court to prevent the sale of her father's 2,700 acre estate. She often spent time in her family summer homes such as the Vanderbilt Mansion in Newport. Doris Duke did a lot of traveling, learned to speak about 9 different languages, and was known to sweat, "hustle," and work hard. She was known to handle her business.

"Game" and "Business" is used so loosely and carelessly. If a man gives money to a woman with a boyfriend or husband for sex and she is not in the business, he doesn't have "Game" HE PLAYED HIMSELF! If a female drop her kids off with her mother or pay a baby sitter while she go have sex with some one she met at the club over the weekend or in a coffee shop during lunch Tuesday, then she's not taking care of business though that is a favorite phrase of "bootleggers". "I'm going to handle some business" when actually she responding to a "booty call".

Doris married twice during her life; first to Jams H.R. Cromwell who later became the U.S. Ambassador to Canada as a result to being married to Doris. Her second marriage is told as if she had more power than Don Corlioni in the <u>God Father</u>. It is said that she met and married Porfirio Rubirosa, (a known playboy) as his third wife, but, he was already married, Doris made Porfirios' wife an offer that she couldn't refuse; 1,000,000 for her husband to get an uncontested divorce. THAT IS DIVA BUSINESS! Remember: A Diva doesn't have to be a gold digger, she already has her own.

Pamela Beryl Digby Churchill Hayward Harriman

Pamela Beryl Digby was born in 1920. Her dad was from an old established family and her mother was the daughter of Baron Aberdare, who was in the House of The Lords. When Pamela was in her 20's, she spent time in England where she soon met Lady Olive Bailey (Rich American Woman) who taught her more about "class" and fine art. She also introduced Pamela to a different life and different men such as Clark Gable, Douglas Fairbank, and Max Beaverbrook. At the castle owned by Lady Olive Bailey is where Pamela Digby starts to learn her identity, role, and her talents as a woman and a caregiver to wealthy men that was emotionally starving. To seek men with money, the mission must be to seek, find, and financially rape and abandonment. Beaverbrook and Pamela were convenient for each other during her young adulthood.

While in England and Europe Pamela met and married Randolf Churchill, the son of Winston Churchill. While Pamela was pregnant with their and only son "Winston"; Randolph was being sent to Cairo because he had became a nerve racking alcoholic (having the son of a Churchill put her on a whole different level). Now Pamela Churchill, she was introduced to Averell Harriman, the heir to the Union Pacific railroad wealth and status. Pamela Churchill knew that Averell was married, away from his wife and could use the attention that she had to offer. The affair last through-out the war. While still married, Pamela Churchill had and affair with another rich American name Jock Whitney, as well as Bill Paley (founder of CBS television). Whitney and Paley later became brother-in-laws by marrying two of the Cushing sisters ("Babe Paley"). Pamela Churchill started having an affair with Edward Murrow. Pamela wanted Murrow to leave his wife, as a business woman; Pamela Churchill understood that the men she decided to attract had important careers that they protected and she should do the same. She understood most of the men had wives at home and the wives basically know that other women was involved but if she was the wife; the one that somehow beat the rest, she would be "locked in", assumes her position played her role and accepted the challenges and competitors for gaining a wealthy man. Pamela Churchill was "on fire"; her next affair would be with Gianni Agnelli, the heir to an automobile fortune. Pamela even converted to Catholicism hoping that would help her chances of him marrying her; He never did. Pamela Churchill had become familiar with wealth, but she experiences the epiphany of wealth when she met Baron E. Rothchild, he was part of the most powerful family in France. They owned vineyards that produce Lafitte-Rothschild wines, and owned banks. Baron Rothschild was also married but he provided Pamela with the finer things that life had to offer for many years. The affair was not a big secret, Rothschild wife simply looked the other way. She knew the "business" and played her part to maintain her starting position. Over time, Pamela (still) Churchill, had affairs with

Stavros Niachros, a Greek shipping magnate, and Prince Aly Kahn, the son of the world's Muslim Spiritual leader, Aga Kahn.

As Pamela Churchill approached forty years old, she and Randolph got a divorce. Around 1955 Pamela moved to New York. A certain society of married women wasn't please to hear that Pamela Churchill would be moving in the circumference of their stalked, haunted and captured husbands. Pamela was definitely a spoken and unspoken threat to wealthy house wives. While out for a night of socializing with the Whitney's, Pamela Churchill met the husband of "Slim Hayward" who was out of town, her husband name was Leland Hayward. (Broadway Producer) Hayward and Pamela Churchill had an affair until Hayward divorce was settle and they could marry each other. Leland died in 1971 with not much money. Running out of money and on a mission, Pamela's old flame from war time, ("Averell Harriman") wife died the same year and they were re-united even, 20 years her senior, Pamela became Pamela Beryl Digby Churchill Hayward Harriman. Averell Harrimas was a respected politician and still Union Pacific heir. In the political world, his resume was nice, he had been; the National Security advisor during Korean War, Governor of New York, State, negotiated Vietnam Peace Talks, Ambassador to Great Britain and Russia as well as Secretary of Commerce under Franklin D. Roosevelt. Pamela became more involved with politics after noticing the Republican Party increasing in power during the early 1980's. With Pamela's help, the Political Action Committee was introduced. Pamela started making public speeches. The (PAC) allowed the democrats to raise money. Pamela spoke in 1984 at the democratic national convention, Harriman health started to get worse, Harriman died, leaving Pamela Churchill Hayward Harriman his entire 110 million dollar fortune.

Just as Pamela's pursuit of a wealthy man, she would not stop working until her efforts would help elect a democratic president. In 1992, the PAMPAC raised over 12 million dollars to ensure a victory for the Democratic Party and the democratic governor of Arkansas; William (Bill) Jefferson Clinton.

In 1997 while swimming for exercise; Pamela Beryl Digby Churchill Hayward Harriman had a stroke and drowned. Bill Clinton and Tipper Gore were in attendance at her funeral. THIS IS THE LIFE OF A DIVA.

A host of young women has had no idea; the thoughts, choices, decisions and actions carried out by a true 100% diva. The following list will clear up some mistaken identities and distinguish Business women and Divas from bootleggers and bored-broke females.

Remember: No matter what type of **HEAD** that a female has, action heroes' are not divas. They write tell-all-books Caught on tapes and is not a DIVA

- Pamela Anderson: on tapes with Tommy Lee and Bret Micheals

- Daniela Cicarelli: on tape with Renat Tato

- Joanie Laurer (Chyna) on tape wit Sean Waltman (X PAC)

  Nichole Narain: on tape with Colin Farrel

42

-

- Carolyn Murphy: on tape with Jake Schroeder

- Tonya Harding" on tape with Jeff Gillooly

- Ulrida Johnson: on tape with Stan Collymore

- Jenna Lewis: on tape with Travis Wolfe

- Jayne Kennedy: on tape with Leon Isaac Kennedy

- Jenni Rivera

- Abi Titmuss

- Jessica Sierra

- Paris Hilton

ACTRESSES THAT ARE DIVAS

- Elizabeth Taylor

- Grace Kelly

- Jean Harlow

- Claudette Colbert

- Lucille Ball

- Kay Francis

- Lisa Raye

- Judy Garland

- Liza Minnelli

- Vivien Leigh

SINGERS THAT ARE DIVAS

Beyonce Knowles

- Sarah Brightmain

- Patti LeBelle

- Mary J. Blidge

- Dianna Ross

- Maria Callas

- Montserrat Caballe

- Whitney Houston

- Billi Holliday

- Cher

- Dolly Parton

- Norma Shearer

- Dilida

BUSINESS WOMEN THAT ARE DIVAS

- Princess Margret

- Oprah Winfrey

- Margret Thatcher

- Eleanor Roosevelt

- Jackie Kennedy

- Imelda Marcos

- Eva Peron

- Hilary Clinton

- Michelle Obama

Artist: **Beyonce**
Song: Diva

"I'm a a diva (hey)
I'm a I'm a a diva (hey)
I'm a I'm a a diva (hey)
I'm a I'm a a diva
I'm a I'm a a diva (hey)
I'm a I'm a a diva
I'm a I'm a a diva (hey)
I'm a I'm a...

Na na na diva is a female version of a hustla
Of a husla
Of a of a hustla
Na na na diva is a female version of a hustla
Of a husla
Of a of a hustla

Stop the track, let me state facts
I told you give me a minute, and I'll be right back
Fifty million round the world and they said that I couldn't get it
I done got so sick and filthy with benj's I cant spend
How you gone be talkin shit?
You act like I just got up in it
Been the number one diva in this game for a minute
I know you read the paper, the one that they call a queen
Every radio round the world know me
Cause that's where I be

I'm a I'm a a diva (hey)
I'm a I'm a a diva (hey)
I'm a I'm a a diva (hey)
I'm a I'm a a diva
I'm a I'm a a diva (hey)
I'm a I'm a a diva
I'm a I'm a a diva (hey)
I'm a I'm a...

Na na na diva is a female version of a hustla
Of a husla
Of a of a hustla
Na na na diva is a female version of a hustla
Of a husla
Of a of a hustla

When he pull up, wanna pop my hood up
Bet he better have a six pack, in the cooler\

Getting money, divas getting money
If you aint getting money then you aint got nothing for me
Tell me somethin (tell me somthin)
Where yo boss at? (where yo boss at?)
Where my ladies up in there that like to talk back?
(that like to talk back)
I wanna see ya (I wanna her her)
I'd like to meet cha (I wanna meet her)
What you said (not to me)
She aint no diva (she aint no diva)

Na na na diva is a female version of a hustla
Of a husla
Of a of a hustla
Na na na diva is a female version of a hustla
Of a husla
Of a of a hustla

Since fifteen in my stilettos been strutin in this game
Whats yo age was the question they asked when I hit the stage
I'm a diva, best believe her
You see her, she getting paid
She aint callin him to greet her
Don't need him , her bed's made.

This is a stick up stick up
I need them bags uh that money
A stick up stick up
You see them ask where that money
All my ladies get it up
I see you I do the same
Take it to another level, no passengers on my plane

I'm a I'm a a diva (hey)
I'm a I'm a a diva (hey)
I'm a I'm a a diva (hey)
I'm a I'm a a diva
This is a stick up stick up
I need them bags uh that money
stick up stick up
You see them ask where that money

Na na na diva is a female version of a hustla
Of a husla
Of a of a hustla
Na na na diva is a female version of a hustla
Of a husla
Of a of a hustla

I'm a a diva
I'm a I'm a a diva x 14
I'm a I'm a a diva (hey)"

Chapter 5

TERMS and DEFINITIONS
Good Words

Prostitution: to sell the services of sex. Prostitution is said to be the "world's oldest profession" (business), illegal in many countries and varies in certain counties in Nevada.

Prostitute: is an individual who <u>charges money or exchange goods/services for performing sexual acts</u>. Other names that relate to prostitutes are: "HOOKER", "WHORE", "CALL GIRL" more recently; porn stars, phone sex operators, escorts, exotic dancers, strippers are classified as prostitutes.

"John", Trick", "Client", "Punter", "Hobbyist", and "Monger" are a few terms used to describe the people who <u>pay for</u> these sexual services.

Brothel: Places used for prostitution, also known as: **Bordellos, Bagnios, Bawdy houses,** and **Cathouses.**

PIMP: defined by most U.S. States laws as anyone who takes a cut of a prostitute's earnings. At times they offer protection and other services to a sex worker.

Madams: are generally known as a female pimp sharing the same responsibilities as a male pimp, the female that heads a house of prostitution.

Dame: title given to a woman of authority (madam) or the mistress of a household.

Groupie: An admirer of a celebrity who attends as many of his or her public appearances as possible. Often celebrities have to hire security to be protected from groupies. Groupies are also attracted to authority figures such as: Ministers, Medicals Doctors, sometimes even convicted criminals have followers. Groupies have a long standing reputation for being available for sex. Opposite of a prostitute, a groupie may have sex for no <u>exchange of money</u>. (She has no business doing such a thing). A groupie may find herself five states on tour for a few days before she gets a bus ticket back home or simply get left by the celebrity. Men tend to not respect women that are so easy and free. Easy and free can't be trusted. Groupies are known to demystify sex: they accept it as physical, and they aren't possessive about their conquest.

Hip Hop Models: females who appear in mainstream rap music videos, magazines, calendars, and other media. Most hope to cross into mainstream T.V and magazines.

Bottom Whore: Pimp or Madam Main Girl, foundation, been around the longest.

Breaking Luck: business woman's first "trick" of a working day.

Chilli Pimp: small time, one whore pimp.

To pull someone's coat: to inform, to teach.

Freedom: this is a political right. Freedom is not a guarantee. Freedom is also: liberation from restraint or from power of another, boldness of conception or execution, and the absence of necessity, or consultant in choice or action.

Live: to be alive, to maintain one-self, to have life and rich experiences, to experience first hand, to exhibit vigor, gusto, or enthusiasm(hustle).

Hustle/Hustler: to convey in a hurried manner. to gain by energetic effort rapidly, to act aggressively in business dealings.

Money: a medium that can be exchanged for goods and services and is used as a measure of their values on the market including forms of commodity. Assets and property considered in terms of monetary value.

Commerce: is a division of trade or production that deals with the exchange of goods and services from producer to final customer. It involves the trading of something of economic value such as goods, services, information or money by two or more people, intellectual exchange or social interaction.

Trade: the business of buying and selling, the exchange of one thing for another.

Sell: to give up (property) to another for something of value (as money), to give up on return for something else.

American: a native or inhabitant of America, a citizen of the United States.

Business: the purchase and sale of goods and services in an attempt to make a profit. Any particular occupation or employment engaged in for livelihood (hustle) or gain, a profession, financial dealings; buying and selling.

Industry: is the manufacturing of a good or service within a category. Industry is a broad term for any kind of economic or financial production.

Crime: an act committed in violation of the law prohibiting it, a criminal act that may be punishable death, imprisonment, or the imposition of certain fines or restrictions.

Victimless Crime: a crime that directly harms no person or property except that of the consenting participants.

Criminal: someone found guilty of a crime.

Dreams: A state of abstraction, a wild fantasy or hope.

Fantasy: An imagined event or sequence of mental images, such as a daydream, usually fulfilling a wish or psychological need.

Sex: All of the feelings resulting from the urge to gratify sexual impulses, the properties that distinguish organisms on the basis of their reproductive role.

Gold Digger: a woman who associates with or marries a rich man in order to get valuables from him through gifts or divorce settlements.

Business is Money
We use the word Business and the phrase "Handle Business" so loosely. Even females are using that term in referring to stepping out on her man. She may tell the baby sitter that she's "going to take care of some business." This may be true for the older playettes; that knows how to handle business and come home with more money than they left with. We will discuss this topic further in the book.

Unfortunately some of us have to lose ourselves before we find ourselves. We forget what is important and that America is a capitalist society. We can't forget to acquire and **save money**.

Since business is money, we can all think of business men with money: No doubt; Jay-Z, Russell Simmons, Don King, Bill Gates, Etc. In 1992, I was in college making about 4,000 a week from hustling. A friend of mine was in the same line of work except he was making about 30,000 a week. I remember asking him one weekend; was he going down to Myrtle Beach S.C. for "Black Bike Week" his reply was "hell no, I ain't got no business down there, I can't do nothing but spend more than I make." He had nice cars, trucks, motor cycles, clothes but it meant nothing to show it off. He rallied behind chasing paper, and from such experiences I was inspired to keep "chasing paper", attracting women and taking care of business. Not being in jail is a major HUSTLE; break the law only when necessary. You can't get money locked up.

PLAYER (Game)
A player of a game is a participant there in. Normally there are at least two players in a game in most games, one player (or team) is declared the winner, the player who perform the best.

It's important to remember; most games have different rules and some games have no rules. "Play fair but Play to WIN"

Game has been tested from the beginning of play. The only way to test game is against game. (Sex a business woman for no money) it is rather easy to mistreat someone that doesn't know they're being mistreated. You are not testing your game. You must challenge your game against the game of a "player" for real. This is how you pick up on things you never thought about or has over looked. The experience is scary but successful. For players with strong minds, this may decide the difference between love, sex, marriage and money.

LIES, the Offspring of Reality
Lie: A statement known to be false and misleading to deceive or give false impression.
Derail: To change the subject matter in order to avoid the truth.
Confuse: to deliberately quibble a subject matter in order to mislead.
Lies of omission: is to remain silent to with hold important information. The silence could be seen as telling a straight-out lie. Preachers, politicians, and celebrities are

very familiar at this style of lying. Sometimes when a person morals or ethics are being questioned, they will consciously remain silent. To not tell on yourself isn't frowned upon according to some. Others believe that silence only intense the deception and is more misleading causing un-measurable grief and misery, example; "Casey Anthony" story.

People lie about doing real things and real emotions. Lies are the barrier to necessities like truth.

This is why women marry, this is why they cheat. Lying is certainly a crucial and important factor of "The Game".

WHY LIE?

Sometimes, you have to lie in order to get the most enjoyment out of life. A person must be able to lie in order to survive and live. Sometimes, you have to lie if it's only to yourself. You know, those tough times when it's really hard and you really aren't sure what the future will bring but yet you tell yourself and your family that everything will be okay. Sometimes a lie is the only escape from reality or the only motivation one may have to offer. For the hustlers and business people that wake up every day and go to work in hopes of reaching Oprah, Bill Gates, Michael Jordan success; must be delusional, major liars, brilliant, lucky or maybe a combination. A lie can be a recreation, a solace, a refuge in a time of need, the tenth Muse, the fourth Grace, mans best and surest friend. Lying is a necessity of your circumstances. If you meet a person that says that they don't lie just remember that: Children and fools speak the truth. The deduction is simple—adults and wise persons hardly speak it. Everybody lie in one way or another. No one could live with a habitual truth teller and no one has to. For a person to think they never lie, he or she is ignorant. People lie to you every day. A lie is sometimes nothing more than a persons' wish for the future.

A lot of younger business women and bootleggers really interrupted what was known as "The Game" because they had no understanding of the psychology of their lies and the effect they would have on the game. Most tricks didn't just start tricking; in fact, "tricks" are getting older thanks to hard work, smart investments and Viagra. However, a lot a business women are younger, dumber and does not stand a chance to get maximum profit from an experienced trick. What chances would a young, ignorant, uncultivated liar have against an experienced expert? The same hold true for an experienced "business woman" verses a new "trick" or unsuspecting civilian.

People that lie all of the time about any and everything, does not really think a lot of self presentation. If they don't know how and when to represent themselves, people will misrepresent you, eventually. This type of liar is bad for business. This liar actually believes himself/herself to be convincing and is very sociable (always talking). A person that lies all the time for no reason can be a pathological liar which may come from mental problems. If you or someone that you know is a pathological liar; you may qualify to get a check every month. Rather it seems good or bad; it pays to lie. Some lies are intended to save time, money or spare emotions. It's important to understand if you are being lied to for acceptance or for rejection. Remember that a lie has to compliment the time of the lie. If there is such a thing as, the perfect lie, then it should come out sounding like and orchestra. It must have the right rhythm, timing and beat. A good liar has to be charming.

Liars benefit everyday in America and you are the subject to a lie every day, brace up and prepare your defense. Women have a lie going around today that men simply don't think to double check. "That's my brother!" Females are bringing their lovers and sex partners into other relationships under the assumption of being biological relatives. Now days, females are describing irresponsible "jump-offs" as their brother and "homeboys".

- A lie of **Convince**: often given by a lazy person

- **Mean and Cruel** lies are mostly formed from resentment

- A **Calculated** lie normally ends with the liar profiting.

- Lies of the conceited often derive from insecurity.

Every woman is different but women often share the same dreams, goals and past realities. There happens to be similarities as to; **Why women get married?** Since men have such big egos and likes to believe that his woman is different than all the rest; here is really why she got married:

- To be happy

- She loves him

- To be free from parents

- To be free from ex

- Because of pregnancy (children)

- **FOR MONEY**

- Companionship

- **SEX**

- Lonely

- It's a good look

WHY WOMEN CHEAT:

- For attention neglected to be given by her husband

- For validation (feel attractive)

- It's exciting

- **SEX**

- **MONEY**

- Revenge

- Insecure

- Unhappy

- Excitement

Some of these reasons, causes and excuses have nothing to do with the man she is cheating on. The business is; knowing to walk away from such situations that may cause him trouble and cost time or money.

The first date is time to pay close attention to someone's character and body languages. There are signs that indicate deception such as:

- Covering the mouth may indicate that the liar feels guilty

- Nervous hand movements

- Rubbing eyes or neck

- Licking the lips

- Will appear defensive

- Delayed expressions

- Actions and expressions does not match body language

If you are engaging in conversation with someone that you believe to be lying; quickly change the subject. A liar will follow the conversation to another subject and may appear relieved to be rescued.

Lies have caused many people much pain, confusion, grief and anger. It may be impossible to figure out why someone told you a particular lie, the reasons may seem very complex but the foundation of any lie is built around fear, greed, hatred and vanity. It is important to assemble yourself a "Truth Team" this is the team where each player is always consciously honest with each other as an investment towards a better, more perfect and more understanding life and profitable life.

The underground world of pimps, hoes, prostitutes and tricks are actually a world with rules, orders and government, that the average mom, dad, sister, brother, aunties, uncles and the average civilian wouldn't even know how to begin to understand this world unless you are a business person, a capitalist.

At the top is the pimp who runs the business. Under him is the "**bottom girl**" she acts as a manager keeping the other girls focused. On occasions when the pimp is away she may gather the money from the other girls and put it all in one stack, as a co-manager and for more surveillance, the pimp may dedicated similar responsibilities to his second favorite girl.

Pimps share unspoken respect towards one another. The least respected is the "**pop corn**" "**pimps**" newer pimps, "**wanna-bees**" and **Hustlers "Gorilla Pimps"** resorts to violence and intimidation for source of control. Pimps that use psychology to intrigue younger business women are called "**Finesse Pimps**" and successful established pimps are known as **players**.

Important to the pimp business is having a selection of girls. Rules allow "B.W." to move freely from pimp to pimp by "**choosing**" the hoe will let the new pimp know that she likes him, if he accepts her money, the money exchange known as "**Breaking bread**." The new pimp let the old pimp know that he just got "peeled" ("yo bitch chose me"). Hoes that move from pimp to pimp is called "**choosey Susie**".

Pimps are known to have "pimp sticks" two coat hangers wrapped together. Pimp kanes are used for the purpose of bringing order. "B.W." can get punished for "**reckless eyeballing**" looking at another pimp.

THE WORD "PIMP" IS OF UNKNOWN ORIGIN - MOST OF US ARE FAMILIAR WITH THE TERM

Pimp through the stereotype of inner-city PIMP was made popular in the 1970's tied to the swagger which was popular among African American men

CAN YOU BE A PIMP?

Not only does **IT** have to be in you, you have to be a thinker, you have to brilliant. It's basically all psychology, psychological warfare patience and timing. That's all part of the life and school of pimping because, like everything, one must grow and continue to move. After having personal dealings with so many different females, the next move for a player pimp is to open a strip club or three and charge each girl 20-100 tip-out every day.

Can you watch your homeboy or brother, do your girlfriend or your wife while you watch her love every minute and every inch of it, then gets up, hand you the money along with a hug. Can you handle it? Ladies, the next time your dude yells out he's a pimp, why don't you ask him is he really a pimp? Once he sees his girl get "beat-up" and he lives through it, he may have a chance.

THINGS TO KNOW

Remember: A typical guy will fool around with his homies girl. Stay away from him! If she doesn't respect you, you don't need her

- when a man is dutiful to a woman, then she has no choice but to respect, honor and love him

- you protect what you value

- land is the basic of all economic security

- No matter what you do out in the world, if you don't have an effective home life then you have nothing.

- be careful who you get pregnant

- associations are critical

PIMPING IS ILLEGAL IN MANY COUNTRIES

The word pimp is sometimes like a verse out of a Holy book. It depends on a person's perception of a pimp, the ears that hear a pimp and the tongue that responds. People tend to say a little of everything when referring to a pimp.

Pimps are known to find and manage clients for business women in order to profit from their earnings. Typically, a pimp don't force "B.W." to stay with him, though some are abusive to keep their "B.W." in pocket, (in check) to get money. A pimp offers protection to his "B.W." from rival pimps, clients and other "B.W.", like a husband wife relationship.

In a marriage, the husband responsibility is to provide security; emotionally, psychologically, morally, spiritually, financially, physically, etc.

Most people that have careers as pimps are usually men. Sometimes you see women in this capacity but rarely involved with street prostitution. Women that manage other women are commonly referred to as mamas or madam.

Locally you will most likely encounter **low level pimps** that present themselves as lovers, or father-figures to girls (who may be runaways or lack family network) before introducing them to prostitution and perhaps "pimp-hoe" relationship can be abusive with psychological intimidation, manipulation and sometimes physical force to control the **stable** (number of girls).

- Bootleggers, you will find everywhere: church, amusement parks, chat-line, internet, supermarket, night clubs, etc. Normally they have little confidence but, audacity to ask for money however they will have sex first, too proud to ask but rather hint around to buy her a drink, take her out, help pay a bill, and look down on females in the "sex industry". Some think they have all the sense.

Chapter 6

Pay to Play
(Enter at own risk)

Men should remember that you don't have to have a lot of money to attract a "Gold digger", "Diva", "Stripper" or a "Bootlegger" but, you have to know what "The Business is". Distinguishing one from another is part of the "Business of The Game". Looking, listening, and proper responses are key elements of the business.

- Ask the right questions at the right time.

- Be a problem solver (short solutions)

- Don't talk too much (be wisely honest)

- Be able, willing and prepared to be lied to, put up with B.S. and listen to stories that will make you insane if you can't tune them out. This is a job, real business. It has proven to be profitable.

- Do and say things that are "surprising" the opposite of what she expects of you take a chance on her never speaking to you again, if she speaks to you then you can test your limitations (wisely)

Men also have to remember that it is not only "Business women" that is seeking to get paid for their time but, the unexpecting school teacher, choir director, neighbor, class mate etc. These women specialty is playing innocent, hiding behind titles, family names and is known as BOOTLEGGERS. They are not real with themselves or others. Business men often fall victim to bootleggers by trusting them. Bootleggers don't comprehend that "Game" has to be tested against "Game" not against the average unexpecting "Joe". When dealing with a bootlegger it is important to remember that her position is that of a player and someone has to loose. You must counter-act a bootlegger. When she lies, you lie ten times more but it is never safe or advised to deal with lies therefore, **RUN!** If not, a bootlegger has time to plan and calculate without being discovered.

- Don't marry her.

- Don't date her.

- Don't get her pregnant.

- Don't have sex with her

If you do or it's already too late then; become familiar with the following terms:

"Game" is commonly referred to having the ability to convince or to persuade someone to see or do things your way. "Game" is the opposite of good business; "Game" is bad business. Business is: any occupation, employment, or task that a person engages in for livelihood. A business man is easy prey for a "player", business men tend to take care of business and "keep it moving". Players, play games with other people livelihood (business), which is serious business. Sometimes, this is the reason for a "contract"; to ensure that each party obeys the terms of the agreement.

Time is often taken advantage of when it comes to taking care of business and getting money. Don't allow other people to waste your time which interferes. Women have been lying and wasting men time for hundreds of years. Women have been and still are browsing the streets, Arenas, churches, etc. looking for a man to take care of her and her children. In most states in America, it is illegal to buy or sell the services of sex **unless** you enter a **contract** (marriage) and receive a license for participation in "The Game" which evens the score from jump ball to 50% to 50% (half). No matter how much money the woman comes into the "Game" (business) with, at marriage, she shares his money and assets. Once the man makes her pregnant, the "ball is in the other court", "it's a rap", if the marriage doesn't work, he stands to loose, if he cheats then both females can sue him.

Sometimes a man will lie not realizing that it is not necessary. When a man meets a woman, he can admit that he has a girlfriend or wife because if she likes him, she will become involved with him regardless. The type of woman that gets involved with a man that is currently in a relationship has a special quality about her that often derives from pain or secrets. This is the type of lady that is in search of guidance and is willing to accept proper guidance. She respects and looks forward to the honesty. Keeping it real with such a lady could prove to be profitable. The man should let her know that he is happy with his current relationship but is willing to "kick it" with her with absolutely no drama. In fact, he has so much to loose that he can only "kick it" with her if she is willing to contribute to his maintenance and livelihood, as well as be nice to his girlfriend or wife. There is no need for drama; they both want to see him do well. The next step is risky and requires the exact right words at the right time; ask his mate is she willing to accept another girl helping them financially. (Everyone knows that he's going to have to have sex with the woman in order to continuously get money from her). For a man that is willing to cheat on his girlfriend or wife; he should cheat with a woman that has money and can help him or with a single female willing to be a stripper to get lots of money to help him. It really doesn't make sense to cheat with someone that you don't benefit from besides the sexual pleasures.

- When a man has a girlfriend or wife, and simply compliment a young lady with a lot of money for her time on a date then, he is looked at as a "John" or "Trick" and looses his job and faces jail time.

- When a man has two girlfriends and is honest with each one, they may decide to agree to share a relationship with the same man. As a family he is the leader, when he starts receiving all of their money for bills etc. he may be considered a pimp and could face jail, or social suicide.

Alimony should be in every man mind before getting married. Alimony is simply maintiance or spousal support when you are not with your spouse. Although, men normally pay alimony, women are also subjected to paying Alimony (Brittany Spears)

Child Support is another very important word that should remain in the vocabulary of men. Child support is when one parent is required to contribute to the support of his or her child or children through the court system.

If a man could possibly escape alimony and child support, he can still get caught-up in "the game" with a word call Palimony. **Palimony** is similar to Alimony except, a woman can still get half just from living with him for a long period of time without marriage as long as they shared a responsibility aside from sex. You know... light bill, washing each others clothes etc.

The following is an example of CHILD SUPPORT situations for some men.

P. Diddy was reported to be paying child support to three different women:

- $21,800 a month to ex-girlfriend Misa Hylton-Brim for their son. This did not include his son's health insurance, vacations, clothes or tuition. P. Diddy didn't start off paying as much child support until Misa requested a court hearing asking for more money and won.

- $12,000 a month to Kim Porter whom Diddy share a child with. Kim doesn't solely rely on Diddy for income.

- $25,000 a month plus medical expenses for the child he share with Sarah Chapman. Diddy was paying the highest amount of child support in N.Y. history.

Russell Simmons was said to reach an agreement with Kimora Lee to pay her 20,000 per child (two) until the two daughters reaches the age of 19 and a half or until the girls A.) Join the military B.) Get married C.) Move out by them selves to start a career. Also, once the girls are old enough to drive, Russell must spend at least 60,000 to buy or lease the girls a car every twenty-four months.

"50 Cent" (Curtis Jackson) was paying 25,000 a month in child support until Shaniqua Thompkins, (his baby mother) started hustling backwards, she rewinds her profits to receiving 6,700 a month. Shaniqua Thompkins is a prime example of the new generation of "players" (fumblers).

Charlie Sheen was reported paying $52,000 a month in child support to Denise Richards for their two daughters and had to pay Richards $60,000 a month in alimony for two years.

It's reported that **Danny Bonaduce** reportedly agreed to share over $6 million dollars in cash and assets with Gretchen Bonaduce right down the middle. Gretchen is the mother of two of Danny's children as well as his ex-wife. Once both parties left the table after the divorce; Gretchen had $3.3 million while Danny left with $3.2 and a monthly child support responsibility of $16,000 per month.

WIN-WIN-WIN

There are a lot of men with a lot of money in America. For a lady to marry, have sex or a baby with such a man, instantly makes her a winner in American society. Some of the men are famous and some not so famous but yet prey and victims. When the man is wealthy, regardless of the out-come of the relationship, love ship, business ship, or friendship; the woman stands to get paid from sharing the truth or sharing lies, she will benefit through marriage, child or even just writing a "Tell All" book. There are professions that attract groupies, gold diggers etc. and the Hip-Hop profession sure has its share of females trying to be in the right place at the right time. The following is a list of high profile Hip-Hop targets because they have more money than the average Hip-Hop entertainers, any story or scandal will sale with their involvement.

- Jay-Z reported to have over $500,000,000.

- P. Diddy reported to have over $350,000,000.

- Russell Simmons reported to have over $350,000,000.

- "50 Cent" reported to have over $200,000,000.

- Pharell Williams reported to have over $200,000,000.

- Nelly was reported to be worth close to $100,000,000.

- Jermaine Dupri is expected to be worth $100,000,000. In America, getting money is not always that difficult, but saving the money and not letting it all slip away seems to be the hard job.

Chapter 7

TRICK BUSINESS

This is an emergency!!! STOP!!! I really wish it was that simple. Reason is: some men don't have a clue that they are "TRICKS". If a man can relate to the following example then, he is a "Trick". He meet a young lady and set up a first date, to prepare for the date, he will:

1.	Go to the barbershop	$18.00
2.	Get his car detailed	$25.00
3.	Pair Jeans	$60.00
4.	Shirt	$30.00
5.	Dinner	$45.00
6.	Movies, popcorn, and drinks	<u>$35.00</u>
		$213.00

$213.00 for a first date and he still didn't buy flowers or candy so, if she don't hold it against him and feels that he deserves to spend more quality time with her for the night then he still has to spend about 65 more dollars for a half decent hotel which brings the date to $278.00 plus the $15.00 in gas. The reason for the hotel room is because taking a first date or stranger into his home is dangerous and suicidal. If the female has things going on and he can benefit from her then the money can be taken as an investment. But for the average man that works a regular job to spend $278.00 of his check while neglecting a bill. Some even neglect paying child support for that one night, that one chance. After spending his check to impress a woman for acceptance, he's likely to be a little tense on the date as the result of him being a "trick" he may never hear from her again, especially if he didn't give her any money.

The reason to refer to men who spend money on females as "Tricks" is because they are being "conned." There can be a group of men standing around talking about positive goals, dreams, ideas, and plans, suddenly a group of females may stride by wearing tightly fitted clothes showing off every curve on their body and the guys will often lose focus of their conversation and one guy yells "DAMN!" after speaking; the lady may respond like she don't even realize how she and her girls are dressed and play like she is offended. She looks in the mirror every morning before leaving home and definitely knows how she looks and what she is presenting. But will fault the guy for not complimenting her for her brains. The guy will try to back tract and start over. STOP!!! Respects, respect, respect; the same female can be dressed fashionable and modest at the same time. Show females the same respect that she may show for herself. If she just don't know any better, then she must be cultivated, (broken down-rebuilt).

"Tricks" are prey to every female. A trick will fall victim to a "Gold digger" a "Business woman" and a "bootlegger". **BE CAREFUL!**

Before Marriage

Anytime a person decides to do business with another person they should apply some factors of future outcome of the decision. Many times before entering into the "business ship" of marriage, a man may be sure to "cover certain grounds" with his fiancé in the direction of a merged future. He may sit her down and review the detailed plans for their future after two or three hours of discussing plans, finances, families, home, hobbies etc. She leaves and he gets on the phone with his college and lifelong friends to assure they get things in place for the up-coming ritual. His friends get to work: BACHELOR PARTY!!!

1.   Find some entertainers

2.   Make reservation payment

3.   Request nudity

4.   Detail description of party location

5.   Type of music that he would like

6.   Request the age(s)

7.   Set time and date

8.   Party Time! "Turn Trick"

And he still loves his fiancé just the same. It's nothing! Should he be charged with a crime for having sex? Why would it matter if he became a politician 15 years later? He only **"paid to play"** for the last time because it supposes to be free for the rest of his life after marriage. Is it free whenever he want it or not if married. Do women get married and expect no financial benefit or are married women really business women?

The day after the most anticipated party of his life, he is then forced to sign a contract promising never to do what he just did less than 24 hours ago. The entertainers that provided the fantasy night got paid and now the bride is about to benefit through marriage or divorce.

THE NEXT DAY (read contract closely)

Sample contract:

"I, _____, take you, _____, as the love of my life. I vow to be patient with you and the circumstances in our lives. I vow to be kind to all people we come across. I vow not to be boastful of our love or about our accomplishments. I promise to be proud of you, but not proud in love for though I will strive for perfection, I know I can never reach it. I promise not to be quick to anger, but to think before I speak and act. I vow not to keep a record of wrongs, but to always keep the happy memories alive. Through God, our love will never fail."

Presbyterian contract:

"_____, wilt thou have this woman/man to be thy wife/husband, and wilt thou pledge thy faith to him/her, in all love and honor, in all duty and service, in all faith and tenderness, to live with her/him, and cherish her/him, according to the ordinance of God, in the holy bond of marriage?"

"I, _____, take you, _____, to be my wedded wife/husband, and I do promise and covenant, before God and these witnesses, to be your loving and faithful husband/wife, in plenty and want, in joy and in sorrow, in sickness and in health, as long as we both shall live."

Episcopal contract:

"_____, wilt thou have this woman/man to be thy wedded wife/husband to live together after God's ordinance in the Holy Estate of matrimony? Wilt thou love her/him? Comfort her/him, honor and keep her/him, in sickness and in health, and forsaking all other keep thee only unto her/him as long as you both shall live?"

"In the name of God, I, _____, take you, _____, to be my wife/husband, to have and to hold from this day forward, for better, for worse, for richer, for poorer, in sickness and health, to love and to cherish, until we are parted by death. This is my solemn vow."

DO NOT SIGN, it's not the 1600's anymore, men don't get his wife possessions, in 2009 and beyond, women are entering into (win-win) marriage situations and leaving with half. Ask Mel Gibson. This behavior is on the increase and the only defense around for it is THE BUSINESS OF GAME.

WHY TRICKS TRICK?

Men spend money to look at sexy girls even more money to receive sexual pleasures. It's been going on for years and the reasons are vast. Besides being raised by women that teach their baby boys to take care of women starting with her and his sister, men "trick" for the fun of it and to some guys, they treat it as a sport; that can have the most women and or spend the most money on them. It's another part of mans competitive aggression. Some tricks get a "rush" from everyone in the club looking at him while he "make it rain" with a couple hundred dollars in ones. Once the rain storm is over, he is more than likely "attacked" by hungry strippers hoping for the promise of more. For some tricks; going to the strip club is as financially dangerous as going to Vegas to gamble or an amusement park; he have no idea if he will walk out of the club completely broke or not. For some tricks, the rush he receives from the attention is addictive.

Every man has his own reason for tricking. Some men can get sex so easy that it is simply no thrill in it anymore because there is no chase involved; it is then much more exciting to spend or give money to a business woman.

Men, if your girlfriend or wife ever compared you to a celebrity wishing that you were more like them now you can show her at least one thing you may have in common with him. Women should remember that the grass isn't always greener on the other side.

Charles Barkley

Charles Barkley is known for being a super star in the NBA. He was pulled over in Arizona and charged with DUI. He told the police that he was in a rush to get some "Head" (oral sex) from a prostitute that he had previously engaged in oral sex with. Barkley said the prostitute gave him the best "blow job" he had ever had in his life.

Jerry Springer

In May 1998, the story about Jerry Springer having sex with the porn star Kendra Jade one day before she appeared on his show with the porn director John Bowen to talk about her 350 person "gang bang" it is said that Springer attorneys reached an agreement with Bowen not to discuss the matter or mention any pay-offs. Prior to that; Jerry Springer was the City Councilman and was forced to resign after writing a check to pay for a prostitute in a Cincinnati brothel. Jerry Springer went on to become the Mayor of Cincinnati and the host of the famous "Jerry Springer Show". Wouldn't it have been a shame for Jerry Springer to have a criminal record for having consensual sex?

Charlie Sheen

Sheen admitted to spending at least $53,000 on the services of prostitutes provided to him by Heidi Fleiss. Charlie Sheen shares the philosophy of many other men and believes that "prostitutes are a time savor compared to other women."

Clarke Gable (1901-1960)

Gable had no "shame in his game". He was an American actor with an appetite for beautiful women even if they cost him. Gable was known to say that; "I can pay (prostitutes) to go away. The others stay around; want a big romance, movie lovemaking."

F. Scott Fitzgerald (1896-1940)

Fitzgerald was an American author that sought his sexual pleasures form a prostitute name Lottie once his wife was admitted into an insane asylum. Lottie gave Francis Scott Fitzgerald confidence and let him know that the size of his penis didn't matter but his experience and skills in the bed is what mattered.

Julius Caesar (100-44 B.C.)

Even Julius Caesar and his soldiers were said to lavish lots of money on prostitutes on their way home from the victorious and successful Gallic wars.

NEWS: the "milonga" dance and the Spanish dance "habanera" were combined by prostitutes and their customers into a very sexy and provocative called the "Tango". Tango is the original dirty dancing and was denounced. Prostitutes were comfortable enough with their sexuality to do the tango.

Babe Ruth

Babe Ruth did not hide the fact that he mingled with prostitutes. When traveling with the Yankees, one of his favorite whore houses (brothels) was "House of Good Shepherd" in St. Louis. In the 1910's and 1920's, prostitutes were sometimes referred to as "sporting girls".

Victor Hugo (1802-1885)
Victor Hugo was an author and wrote "The Hunchback of Notre Dame."
Hugo was known to have a very big appetite for sex. Even his wife gave up trying to satisfy him. Hugo was known to have hundreds of sex partners, prostitutes and mistresses. He was sexually active until his death at 83 years old.

Napoleon I (1769-1821)
Napoleon was the first emperor of France and he had a couple of mistresses, his favorite was said to be Marie Walewska. Though, Marie had an agenda, she wanted Napoleon to help her homeland gain independence. Napoleon Bonaparte admitted that his first sexual experience was with a street walker (prostitute) when he was just 18 years old.

Ernest Hemingway (1899-1961)

Hemingway was an American author and a Nobel Prize winner. He enjoyed and services of prostitutes and would sometimes let them become the basis for the characters in his stories. He would give them names like "Xenophobia" and "Leopoldina".

Warren G. Harding (1865-1923)

Warren G. Harding was the 29th president of the United States. Harding frequented brothels. While a Senator, Harding gave $30.00 for sex to a young college graduate and the daughter of his life long friend, her name was Nan Britton.

Ari Onassis (1906-1975)

Aristotle Socrates Onassis met Eva Paron (Evita) she immediately invited him to her villa on the Italian Rivera. Once Aristotle arrived, Evita immediately made love to him. Before he left the villa, Evita had a $10,000 check to be donated to her favorite charity. The $10,000 is more like $100,000 now. Who ever say the "Game" hasn't changed can not be trusted.

Hans Christian Anderson (1805-1875)
Anderson was the author of "The Little Mermaid" and "The Ugly Duckling". Anderson was known for visiting brothels and paying prostitutes for verbal intercourse. A lot of times, "tricks" just need somebody to talk with and listen to them.

Vincent Van Gogh (1853-1890)
Vincent Van Gogh was a Dutch painter that admitted liking prostitutes because thy accepted him as a fellow out cast. Vincent had a son with one of the prostitutes, her name was Claudia Maria Hoornick, she lived with him for about a year and was the model for several pieces of "Van Gogh" work, he actual had a painting titled "The Brothel".

Lord Byron (1788-1824)
Lord Byron was an English poet and the author of "Don Juan". Byron was attending Trinity College as a wealthy noble man. He rented a palace and let

prostitutes live there all for his enjoyment. Margarita Cogni (one of Byron mistresses) was in charge of the palace while Byron was away living in Venice.

Donald Sterling

Donald Sterling is the owner of the Los Angeles Clippers, admitted to having an affair with a prostitute name Alexandra Castro. Sterling and Castro had to let the courts decide over a matter concerning one of Sterling houses that Castro claims Sterling let her have. This man had to go to court to convince a judge that he didn't give a prostitute his house. Sterling is known in the league to be one of the stingiest owners in the league. Maybe until it comes down to sex.

If the wives and girlfriends are reading this book and is sadly surprise to learn who some famous trick are and don't think that it is right for men to pay women for sex. What do you think about your man getting paid to have sex? Ask yourself this question… would you have sex or enter a relationship with **Sylvester Stallone**? Would you still do it knowing that before he became famous that he landed in a porn film "Party at Kitty and Studs?" That's right; Sylvester Stallone first movie acting role was porn. Sex was only business.

Sylvester Stallone

After interviewing clients and the regular customers of strippers, I ask them, why do they trick? Answers cover a wide range of reasons:

- Poor sex life with partner

- Loss of passion in his relationship

- Some men didn't feel loved by their partner

- Wife is always working or busy

- Partner is not attentive

- Lack of emotional and sexual bond

- Lack of commitment to his partner

- Because of a physical, emotion or sexual abuse

- Just for sex

- Out of respect for his wife or girlfriend (didn't want to offend with certain request)

Some men don't even look at giving women money for sex as a real crime. Many tricks view prostitution as a victim less crime. A victim less crime is illegal and does not involve any intrusion on anyone's personal property. Also, no injured party files a complaint with the police. Victim less crimes include prostitution, gambling and drug usage. All are acts that the party voluntarily participates in.

For the suga daddy's, sponsors and men that have business women as their mistresses is because "Business women" posses the qualities of the perfect partner. The perfect partner will do things like:

- Have his dinner ready when he comes over

- Don't nag him

- Reward him

- Don't complain when he spend time with friends

- Be interested in his interest

- Sex is always available

The Business of Friendship

The friend a person chooses is vital no matter male or female. Lots of decisions are made according to a person's friend's point of view; it could be as simple as a ride to the store. The least a person can do for themselves is have a friend that they can trust to ride with without having anything illegal in the vehicle. Environments influences decisions, it may not be wise to have a lot of friends. The less people that are on your team is the less people that can play against you. It really doesn't take a lot, it take the right ones. If there is a person in your life that by the end of the conversation you are never a beneficiary then, that person is bad business.

It has been proven that friends never have to double date and their girlfriend or boyfriends don't have to meet and be buddies. In fact, the girlfriends and boyfriends of friends should treat each other as brother and sister during their unions and use as few words as possible. Friendship has nothing to do with who you are dating at the time, the rules for marriage varies. The wives meet because the bond between the friend and their mate is permanent. A girlfriend or boyfriend doesn't have as much to loose by trying to move in on friends mate. Friends have to realize that the mate should always initially be viewed as an enemy to the friendship. A lot of good friendships have had major interferences because of it. Besides sometimes the easiest sex to get is from your mate's best friend, or relatives. Ex.)

Sometimes friends have to work and think as one, especially in a bar, restaurant or night club and strip club. Friends have to be able to survive the same interrogation; friends have to know each other. Example.) If you heard that your friend of 15 years was out on the town drinking and being loose but you know your friend don't drink, isn't loose and definitely wouldn't go out without you. There would be no reason to respond, but you should realize that you have just identified your source of information as the enemy of your friend which gives you and your friend an enemy. Most people friends are their peers and are around the same age so; the relationship experience is basically the same. Each friend experience the same things but perhaps in different ways and is also trying to figure out rights, wrongs and solutions so there is really never a reason to go into detail about you and your partners relationship. It is sometimes best to speak with an older, wiser person or simple seek professional counseling. It's not fair to a friend to burden them with a personal issue and not fair to one self by giving their mate to their friend simple from talking too much. When you don't want your friends at your mate, keep your relationship business where it belongs.

No matter what the business is, you have to take care of your business. Games are still being played and sometimes totally unexpecting from a real business man. **Mayor Gavin Newsom** of San Francisco did not commit a crime and was not caught with or soliciting a prostitute. He was not involved with an 18 year old intern. No! What Mayor Gavin Newsom did has been considered worse by some; Newsom had an affair with his friends, wife. His "friend" was also his campaign manager, Newsome was the boss. It is possible that he tactfully made sure that his campaign manager would be away working hard for him while he was working hard on his wife. Never trust smiles and be careful who hands you (slap) shake, Deception is deceiving. A smart businessman with a beautiful wife may shy away from doing business with such a "Gamer", "Player". You should never expect "Good Business" with a "bad man" Newsome has created negative opinions from among others simply from not having loyalty to his friend, as well as a business associate.

How to Improve a Relationship or Love ship
Relationship tips:

1. Be honest

2. Listen with interest. Listen, learn and respond genuinely

3. Learn body language and facial expressions or your mate

4. Don't use your mates tooth brush

5. Know who is who among family and friends

6. Don't socialize with ex's

7. Keep private matters, private

8. Have good hygiene

9. Always deliver more than promised

10. Compliment

11. Monitor their friends and family, who ever don't benefit your relationship, is subject to be on a social time-out.

12. Become or remain your mate's friend. Know when it is appropriate for kissing, hugging and holding hands; the mall is no place to walk around holding hands. Never show public displays of affection, it may be considered disrespect towards each other. Affection is for your pleasure and privacy. Keep your business to yourself.

Important Answers to know in a Relationship/Love ship prior to marriage
You must know the answer to these questions whether you ask them or not:

- Religious Affiliations

- Political Affiliations

- Social affiliations

- Age

- Ever been raped or molested

- Have children, ever had an abortion

- Longest relationship. How long has it been over?

- Ever been intimate with the same sex?

- Ever received money or profited form sex?

- Ever had sex with a friend or relatives mate or partner?

- Ever been a part of a threesome or orgy?

- Weakness

- History of drug use

- Medical conditions

- Education

- Type of person he/she is attracted to?

- Have or had a stalker

- Ever been married?

- Why are certain slow songs his or her favorite?

- Criminal background

- Career goals

- How many prior sex partners?

Some people may be offended to be asked or expected to answer some of these questions, and others may be afraid to ask them but, these questions and answers will definitely have an impact on your relationship/love ship or marriage (your life). You may decide that; the person can't benefit your life and happiness or maybe, you can't provide happiness and fulfillment to their life at the time. Sometimes people are not quit prepared for who they attract. You must be honest and respect their visions and views of life.

The relationship-is the time of dating, and learning to be sure if your invested time will ultimately pay-off. The relationship period may or may not lead to the love ship which would be followed-up by marriage. It is good business to know the right questions to ask. This is the time when communication may be the most important. Take nothing for granted.

T-Pain is the Trick Anthem King

Just to listen to T-Pain lyrics, it is evident that if he believes what he sings then he has to be the world's biggest trick. However, if it wasn't for T-Pain and his unusually cleaver lyrics and sounds, strippers and strip clubs would have really missed out the last couple of years. T-Pain music really motivates strippers and tricks.

I'm In Love With A Stripper lyrics   by T-Payne

[Intro]

"Gd" Lil Mama
U know u thick as hell u know what I'm sayin
Matter fact
After the club u know what I'm talkin bout
Me and my "n"s gone be together u know what I'm sayin
I ain't gon worry bout them really though
I'm just lookin at u
Yea u know
U got them big ass hips god damn!

[Verse 1]

Got the body of a goddess
Got eyes butter pecan brown I see you girl
Droppin Low
She Comin Down from the ceiling
To tha floo
Yea She Know what she doin
Yea yea yea
She doin that right thang
Yea yea yea yea ea
I Need to get her over to my crib and do that night thang
Cause I'm N Luv wit a stripper

[Chorus x2]

She poppin she rollin she rollin
She climbin that pole and
I'm N Luv with a stripper
She trippin she playin she playin
I'm not goin nowhere girl I'm stayin
I'm N Luv with a stripper

[Verse 2 (T-Pain)]
Out of all the girls she be the hottest
Like n the way she break it down I see u girl
Spinnin wide
And She lookin at me
Right in my eyes
Yea She got my attention
Yea yea yea
Did I forget to mention
I Need to get her over to my crib and do that night thang
Cause I'm N Luv Wit a Stripper

[Verse 3 (Mike Jones)]
She's every man's dream
She's God's gift to Earth
Women they love 'em too
That's what you call a women's worth
See I love all the strippers
Because they show me love
They know I never pay as free whenever I hit the club
But I can't even lie
The girls are here so fly
She slidin' up and down that pole got me mesmerized
Mike Jones don't ever trick
But god damn she thick
I can't lie, I must admit
I'm in love with a stripper

[Chorus x2]

[Verse 4]

She can pop it she can lock it
Teddy Penderass down I'm bout to see this sexy girl
In My bed
She don't know what she is doin
To my head
Yea She turnin tricks on me
Yea Yea Yea
She dont even know me
Yea yea yea ea
I'd have got her over to my crib to do that night thing Cause I'm N Luv Wit a
Stripper"

Long Lap Dance lyrics   by T-Payne

Verse 1

"Yeayey. It's 241 toniiight (ooh). Fellas grab my lady, ladies get that money, from
the V.I.P to the main stage. (ooh.whoa.whoa.whoa.whoa.whoa. yeayey.) I never seen
that shawty dooo that(that) on the bong (on the bong) reaching my pocket full of 2
stacks. Get it all (get it all) if you never done this don't you feel dumb with it. Shawty
come over to you start getting it all. Then the song is almost done (the song oh) so I
made a long(long) lap dance song.

Chorus

I need a 241 or something otherwise I need my own lap dance song. I only been with
you in 2 hours and all my dollar bills is gone. For my lap dance song. I moan more
than a minute with you before I spend a minute with you. Girl c'mon don't do me

wrong you know what's goin' on. Yeaah! This is the long lap dance song.

Verse 2

Yeayey. It's 241 toniiight (ooh). Fellas grab my lady and ladies get that money, from the V.I.P to the main stage. (ooh.whoa.whoa.whoa.whoa.whoooa. yeayey.) shawty came out from the main stage(stage) to the floor (floor). They were waitin to the V.I.P (P.got it all)
Baby was so ready hot and so heavy. She got on top of me until the comfort room. And the song is over (the song oh) so I made a long (long) lap dance song. so I made a long(long) lap dance song. *Chorus*

Verse 3

Yeayey. It's 241 toniiight (ooooh). Fellas grab my lady, ladies get that money, from the V.I.P to the main staaage. (ooh.whooa.whooa.whooa.whooa.whooooa. yeayey.) Girl where you goin' you can't leave me here (here) like this (this) girl do you know where at me when you're done lets took my ring (riing). Girl you can't leave me (no) please believe me (no) you gotta stay over here and can't get it at all. Till the song is over baby I know that this is the long lap dance song." *Chorus*

Can't Believe It lyrics   by T-Payne

"(she make me feel so good better than i would by myself or if was with somebody else)
(she make the people say yeah,yeah)

I can put you in the log cabin somewhere in aspen
Girl ain't nothing to the pain and trickin if you got it what you askin....for
Put you in the mansion somewhere in wiscansin (wisconsin)
Like i said ain't nothing to the pain we can change are last name what happnin?
Cause you look so good
tell me why you wanna work here? I put you on the front page of a king magazine, but you gon get yourself hurt here
Eh,baby i bought you in the back just to have a conversation
Really think you need some ventalation
Lets talk about yoooh & meeee

Oh, I can't believe it
oooh oooh she all on me
man,man, i think she want me(want me)
Nah I can't leave her lonely... naww
(x2)
And you don't understand she make the people say yeahhh,yeahhh,yeahhh
She hit the main stage she make the people say yeahhh,yeahhh,yeahhh

I could put you in the condo
All the way up in Toronto
Baby put you in the furcoat ridin the Murciélago
I put you in the beach house
right on the edge of Costa Rica
Put one of em lil flowers in your hair have you looking like a fly mamacita
(fuego)
Cuz you look so good
You make me wanna spend it all on ya
Get up out this club
slide with ya boy
We can do what you wanna Yeah
baby i brought you in the back cuz you need a lil persuasion,
plus you need a lil ventalation
let's talk about youuu and meeeee

Oh I can't believe it
OOh OOh she all on me(on me)
Man Man i think she want me
Nah i can't leave her lonely...naww
(x2)
And you don't understand she make the people say yeahhh,yeahhh,yeahhh
She hit the main stage she make the people say yeahhh,yeahhh,yeahhh,

[Lil Wayne]
Now i can put your ass out ohhh
keep running your mouth
And if yo brothers come trippin ima show em wat dese teardrops fo'
Shawty i was just playing
ohh but i can take you the caymen...islands
and have you screaminn and hollerin
aww then we gone be making...
Love on the beach the people see what we doing
Awww they pointin and moooovin
And ohh but we gone keep on doing....it
Like its just me and you and nobody else
around went down on the balcony,
and I ain't talking no Penthouse Suite,
Shawty like a model out da Penthouse Sheets,
Thats why i got her on ma' Penthouse Sheets.

Oh I can't believe it
OOh OOh she all on me(on me)
Man Man i think she want me
Nah i can't leave her lonely...naww
(x2)
And you don't understand she make the people say yeahhh,yeahhh,yeahhh
She hit the main stage she make the people say yeahhh,yeahhh,yeahhh,"

Chapter 8

Making of the modern woman
(From Then To Now)

In the 1600's Europeans begin arriving in America. European men (white men) seemed to believe that the women were inferior to the men yet was expected to help the men work the fields while maintaining all of her domestic (house) chores. Women and girls were only taught to read in-order to read the bible which would supposedly make them better wives. Coincidently the bible was also forced upon African Slaves as well, perhaps to make them better and more manageable slaves. ("Turn the other cheek when somebody hits you or it's easier to go to Heaven if you are poor") but that's another book.

Single women weren't as restricted (legally) but finding a job was more difficult. The married women could get work a little easier but had few other rights. She was expected to live under a tight marriage contract, romantic and passionate love was hardly a concern. If the woman come from a wealthy family or not; as soon as she said "I do" all of her money and possessions became the property of her husband. From 1600-1800, there was a long period when colonial wives could not speak in public, own property, write a will or even claim her children. To write a book on how many men she had sex with and gave "blow-jobs" to would have been un-heard of.

By the 1920's, women were proclaiming liberation and independence. Women weren't just housewives and helping in the fields anymore, they were: dancing, partying, and wearing revealing clothes. However, some of those females were more rebellious and curious. The true independent women hurried found employment. Though, things had changed, women still faced sexual harassment, low wages, and a hard time when seeking credit (merchant).

Just as African American and Mexican American; women were accused of taking all the jobs from men. Around the 1930's, it began to show that men were leaving there wives to raise the family and become a single mother. After World War II, single working women was becoming recognized and glamorized by the film industry. Around this time is when women was first introduced to benefits such as; minimum wage, social security, and unemployment insurance.

By the 1950's, women were being spoiled, like spoiled brats, (gimme, gimme) women wanted more and begin to taunt authority while becoming more rebellious in the 60's, by the 70's, women had learned their rights and was certainly not neglecting any of them. Women had suffered and learned from it, by the 80's women had learned that they could not only follow but could assist greatly from the leadership and authorative position. By the end of the 1980's; women had choices on abortion and even hurtled themselves into space, and appointed to the Supreme Court, congress, and boards of major businesses.

Women have certainly been liberated since the 1600's. In the 1950's, it was taboo for a woman to perform oral sex on a man unless she was married to him or a prostitute. The wife and prostitute use to be the ones that got the pleasure of giving "blow-jobs" now-a-days, it's (damn near) "free for all."

SAME GAMES-NEW PLAYERS

Now days in America, men are being targeted, arrested, embarrassed and becoming criminals because they had sex with a woman and respect the fact that she may have children and responsibilities and "looked out" for her financially. Men are going to jail for looking out. "Looking out" for females was once accepted by many. The business was different then. The women knew they had mouths to feed and handle their "business". To go and tell that she has had sex with the "mayor" or the "radio personality" of the day would insure that her life as a business woman would be complete. Women knew that selling sex tapes and writing books exploiting the familiar that she would be "hustling backwards". BE QUIT and GET PAID!

If you are familiar with sex, money or politics, then you have probably heard of **Jessica Cutler**. Cutler was born in 1978; she is an author and former congressional staff assistant for Senator Michael DeWine. For some reason, Jessica Cutler published a blog called Washingtonienne and detailed her life, and hers and other sex lives in D.C. on her blog she had

"F"=married man who pays me for sex
"W"=sugar daddy who wants nothing but oral sex
"RS"= my new office BF with whom I am embroiled in an office sex scandal.

By the end of the list she said "shit, I am fucking six guys. Ewwww!" Cutler wrote that she received about $400.00 for sex from a George W. Bush appointee. It made no sense for Cutler to share her sexual encounters in D.C. But it seems that she is in touch with reality. She said; "I am sure that I am not the only one that makes money on the side this way. How can anybody live off $25,000?" After lawsuits of false allegations and so on, Cutler filed bankrupt. Bankrupt is often the result of "Bad Business".

A lot of the younger women do not have the proper understanding of business which in returns, gives "the business" a black eye. There is less or no loyalty anymore. A lot of them would prefer the fame and forfeit the fortune. Tip for up and coming business women is; don't write books, do interviews, post a web page or work for a escort service if you want to be discrete.

Video Vixen **Summer Walker** has been seen and gain notoriety from Lil Jon's video "Snap your finger" was recently said to be caught-up in a prostitution scandal and connected to an escort service based in Atlanta, describing herself as "sexy, passionate, and sweet" with measurements of 36DD-24-35 allegedly called herself Jizel.

Gloria Velez is also known as a video vixen, talking too much and do enjoy sex. Gloria has been known to date Aaron Hall whom she claims to share a baby with and affair with rapper Joe Buddens. Gloria accused both men of being aggressive with her. Gloria plays the character "Animal" on "Luke's peep show". "WOW"!

There may be certain type of people that you would like to stay away from. There was a video vixen and porn star that definitely deserves isolation from the rest of society. This action hero has claimed to sleep with, Bill Maher, Shaquille O'Neal, Lil Wayne, DMX, Diddy, Ice-T, Usher, Bobby Brown, and Vin Diesel. This action hero then goes on to accuse Morgan of trying to run her over with his car and trying to kill her. According to the Palm Beach post, this action hero was pregnant by Bobby Brown. This book only list a short list of her sexual encounters but, you can see that she has no certain preference. It lets you know that she is not a true gold digger "business woman" because she didn't get pregnant by the right one and, if she as a woman has sex with a variety of men with no protection or birth control, she's a nasty Bootlegging Groupie!

The purpose of this chapter is not to "knock" Hip-Hop girls, models and vixens but to show comparisons of the financial out-come of "Game" and "Business". There are some video vixens that understand the business of their assignments and capitalize on the opportunities such as:

MEAGAN GOOD

Meagan Good is another well known video actress/video vixen out of Panama City California. Meagan seems to be making the right connections, being smart and understanding her business. In 2003 or 2004, Meagan and I happen to be hanging out in Charlotte N.C. in 50 Cents dressing room along with "50" and a host of others including G-Unit which seem to be at least 200 guys (exaggerated). In the 21 questions video she was beautiful but in person, she is extremely beautiful though at the time, a little slim (author opinion) she wasn't my type and I wasn't "50" so that worked out well. But since then, she is thicker and hasn't stopped eating. Her plated include K-Ci and JoJo video "This very moment", Will Smith Black suits coming, 50

Cent "21 Questions" the movie "Roll Bounce", "The Cook-Out", "You Got Served", "Biker Boyz", "Deliver Us From Eva" etc. The entertainment business is no game, it is a business. Meagan is doing what many video models only dream of; handling her business.

Lisa Raye McCoy Misick

Lisa McCoy is known as Lisa Raye born in 1967. Lisa has a half sister that is a rapper known as Da Brat. Lisa attended Eastern Illinois University before show business. Lisa Raye has been an inspiration through the realities of life as well as some of her roles on camera. A lot of young African American college women do related to her role as "Diamond" In Player Club as (a college student that turn to stripping to take care of her and her child while she was pursuing a better life, a better career. Stripping was a means to and end). Lisa Raye has done work as a video model for income. She has appeared in "Toss it up" by Sisqo, Lil Jon and Ice Cube "Roll Call" Ludacris "Number 1 Spot" and Tupac's last video. Movies and T.V. appearances are:

- Reason

- In the house

- Parent Hood

- Player Club

- The Wood

- Rhapsody

- Date form Hell

- All About You

- Civil Brand

- Go for Broke

- Love Chronicles

- Gang of Roses

- All of Us

- Super Spy

- Beauty Shop

- Envy

- The Proud Family movie

- Black man Guide to understanding Black women

- Contradictions of the Heart

Lisa Raye lived to become Lisa Raye McCoy Misick after marring the Michael Misick, the Premier of the Turks and Caicos Island. Lisa and Michael divorce was announced in 2008. Lisa Raye is yet one of America's favorite working actresses as well as respected.

Another actress that understands respect and has good business and definitely learns and grew is **Lauren Nicole London** born December 4, 1984. Lauren London has song vocals on Pharrell album "In my Mind" and has appeared in music videos such as "That Girl", "Drop it like its Hot", "Frontin" and many of Pharrell music videos. The list continues; "What you Know" (by T. I.), "Miss Independent" (by Neyo) with Gabrielle Union and Ker Hilson, "Driven Me Wild" (by Common). Lauren London never stopped at videos, London also has made television and movie appearances in: "Everybody Hates Chris", "Entourage", "BET'S RIP THE RUNWAY", "BET'S Top 25 under 25", "The Johnsons", "ATL", and 90210. Lauren gets props for keeping the business moving.

NO GAME (Business Women)

In business, everybody has a role to play, especially when it comes to sex and money. Actress should act, models should model, and video vixens should be in videos, maybe advance to the big screen but not write "Tell All" books and let the pros handle the hoes. Pros always respect, and dedicate themselves to their profession or business. With the economy in 2009 and job lost in America, there is no time for games when there is a "Game" there has to be a winner and a looser. Out of desperation or anxiety to win, people often cheat to "win". Most losses cost time, money or both, its dangerous to be a part of any personal games. To expect to receive money for a sexual service is certainly a business and has been for 100's of years and arguably 100's more. Some say that buying and selling sex is the oldest profession.

Women understand this is business, just ask **Cecil Suwal**, she was 23 when she pleaded guilty to running the day-to-day operations of the FAMOUS former Emperors Club VIP, the same prostitution ring that took down former Gov. Eliot Spitzer. Suwal was sentenced to serve 21-27 months in jail.

"Natalie" McLennan is an aspiring actress from Canada and former #1 prostitute in New York. Actually, Natalie learn and executed her craft well and was known to charge no less than $2000 an hour which also put her to the head of her "prostitution 101 Business Class" Natalie claims to have graduated from the class and become the teacher of Ashley Dupre (call girl in scandal with Eliot Spitzer) and has now written a memoir.

Sydney Biddle Barrows is another female with a nice clue of the business. Sydney was known for being the "Mayflower Madam". She got the nickname because her wealthy older relatives came to America on the Mayflower. Aint that a bitch? That's a little ridiculous, if she was an African American Madam, maybe she would have been known as "Slave Ship Sara" Damn! That's ridiculous but, Barrows escort service was called "Cachet" and based out of New York. "Cachet" serviced the likes of business men, bankers, doctors, lawyers, executives. Barrows ran "Cachet" under the name Sheila Devin. Unlike celebrities and high profile men that never recover from sexual scandals, Barrows is said to be living in New York City and wrote a memoir.

Andreia Schwartz was another young beautiful madam living in America from Brazil. Schwartz was involved in the Emperor's Club VIP escort service. Being a business woman that understands the word business, Madam Schwartz turns down a green card and was rather deported than to "rat" or sell out client #9. (Eliot Spitzer) Andreia Schwartz could have stayed in America a free woman and wrote a book but again, she is a business woman. (Does it seem that writing a "Tell All" book upsets the Author a little?)

Deborah Jeane Palfrey was a 50 year old female known as the D.C. Madam when police searched her Northern California home. At the time authorities froze about 500,000 in assorted stock and bank accounts. Deborah Palfrey had a prior conviction in California for running a prostitution business. After her conviction and paying her debt to society, while sent away to "criminal college" It's suspected that Palfrey did a lot of thinking and planning. After Palfreys 18 month stay in prison, she did her market research as any smart business person would do. She decided on Washington D.C. because D.C. is a liberal, sophisticated, cosmopolitan area. The marketing plan was brilliant. Example: "23 and older, with two or more years of college education, who either work and/or go to school in the daytime," Palfrey's business was treated as such. Those were the type of articles Palfrey ran for advertising.

The name of Palfreys business was Pamela Martin and Associates Escort Service. Investigators say that when hiring a prostitute, the prostitute is tested, to ensure she is not a police officer; the request is to have sex with out getting paid, sort of an initiation ceremony. Palfrey's business women would be requested to work no less than 3 nights a week and was said to charge no less than $300.00 per session. Palfrey and each business woman would share the earnings. As the investigation continued and pressure was building on Palfrey to disclose her "salacious detail" client list but before a trial and after politician had admitted to being connected to her business and resigning, Palfrey was found dead with an apparent suicide note beside her. Rest in Peace "Boss Lady".

THE OLD WAY OF BUSINESS (WHEN BUSINESS WAS BUSINESS)
There has been days when politicians, celebrities, tricks, madams, and business people didn't have to hide, be deported, resign, go to jail or kill themselves because they was accused, caught or admitted receiving money or used sex as a buy and trade commodity. That's when business was booming.

Money for sex was readily accepted by many. New Orleans had the biggest Red-light district in America with no real competitor besides Butte, Montana's' red-light district. Brothels (whore houses) were growing in popularity. The sound of music seeped outside of the windows and door cracks of brothels and America was introduced to Jazz.

Madams (female pimps) in New Orleans were very flamboyant and handle their business fiercely. With knowledge and control of their business, madams would attract business men and couples with the live Jazz music and beautiful women for entertainment, Brothels became a common hang-out and meeting place for business men and couples to go out for an evening out on the town. When business was business, pimps were known as "players" and their responsibility was working in the brothels as agents for the women. A "players" responsibilities included; being sure the women represented the brothel well, was healthy and on time.

In the late 1800's; prostitution was a hot topic in New Orleans. With such high demands, a plan was implicated by city alderman Sidney Bechet. He proposed a section of town (district) where this particular service could be provided, controlled, and out of the way of churches and their congregations. This is why today; strip clubs have to be in a certain zone (depending on state) and so many feet from churches or schools. Stand up and clap for the business man Sidney Bechet and the "Red-light district"

Anna Wilson (Madam) May 27, 1835- Oct. 27, 1911

Famous Lincoln prostitute Josie Washburn worked for Anna Wilson. Anna built a 25 room mansion and another nice home before dying at the age of 76 and was said to be worth upwards of a million dollars. That was a lot of money then.

Sally Standford

Sally Standford (May 5, 1903-Feb. 1, 1982) Mayor of Sausalito, California and a Madam. She was born Mabel Busby. She was the Madam at 1144 Pine Street from 1940-1949 many governor delegates was customers of Sally Standford and they actually had negotiations in the living room of the whore house.

Polly Adler

Pearl "Polly" Adler (April 16, 1900-June 11, 1962) was a Russian born a Madam. "Polly" began to learn the "business" at the age of 19 in New York City once she moved in with a "show girl" she open her first "bordello" in 1920 at the age of 20, under the protection of mobster Dutch Schultz. In 1930, she witnessed the Seabury Commission investigations and fled to Florida to avoid testifying. Adler buried her money in the "underworld" and shifted her whore houses from apartment to apartment for over 20 years. She was said to be a millionaire. That was a lot of money then.

Elizabeth Needham

It is said that Elizabeth Needham died in 1731 also known as Mother Needham; she was an English procuress and brothel-keeper of 18th century London. Her house and life style was notorious for being one of the most exclusive. She was known to be ruthless with the girls. Now-A-Day, she would be considered a "Gorilla Pimp" she would overwork her girls, she may even imprison them. Elizabeth was definitely a scout for talent, her prey was fresh country girls, girls at other brothels, "Bails" where homeless girls lived, she was artful, and she could hide her vicious character until the girls where in her house.

Elizabeth Needham client list included: Colonel Francis Charteris and his cousin Duke of Wharton Charteris. Charteris was later convicted of rape which had nothing to do with Elizabeth Needham business. Sally Salisbury was a prostitute and Charteris mistress at the beginning of her career. Salisbury and another prostitute got Earl of Cardigan's drunk and robbed him of his jewelry and clothes, he played it off as a joke.

AH TOY

The sex for money business isn't quite as new as the internet businesses in fact; it would be extremely difficult to find a business that came before it. That's right! The sex business didn't start with Jessica Cutler, Alexandra Dupri, an action hero or the D.C. Madam. Prostitution dates back at least to the 1800's. Women have received gifts, money, time and attention for their unique services to men. This business would require the right females, some would say the wrong type of lady but whichever way it goes, she arrived to San Francisco California from Hong Kong at the age of 21.

During her trip from China to the United States, she was traveling with her husband until he died on the voyage. She became the mistress of the captain. He "held her down" (took good care) of her by showering her with gifts and gold. By the time they (touched down) had arrived safely to America, Ah Toy was weighed down with gold and an abundance of money. By being overwhelmed and paying attention to the compliments given to her in this new country and new city, she listen and learned from all the compliments that she had been receiving for her beauty in this new city, she decided to capitalize. She decided to have what society grew to call "peep shows" however, the name for the money making racket was called a "lookee". Clients paid one once of gold $16.00 only to see her face for a limited time. This business expanded her entertainment to high price prostitution. As business continued to flourish, Ah Toy expanded her business yet again and opened a chain of brothels and began importing girls from China. It is said that she died a wealthy woman in 1928, 3 months prior to her 100th birthday. American men would like to say thanks to The Business idea of Ah Toy.

Chapter 9

Are You A Business Woman (Exotic Dancer)?

The answer to that question depends on each female. Being a successful exotic dancer has something to do with every aspect of your life. Such as where you come from, your family relationships, your mate, your goals, your future, your ability to be influenced, and your ability to be impressed. A dancer, that use drugs certainly will not maintain as well and as long as a drug free dancer.

Almost any respectable female with common sense can make money as a business woman but, she must have the ability to listen well, respond accordingly, know what to say, when to say it, and which customer to say it too. She must always remember that every customer is different, no matter how he looks and no matter how he is dressed. Now days, you cannot judge a man by his shoes. True hustlers understand that the economy is in a "jam" and if a guy has on "fresh whites" air force ones, then eight out of ten of them has less than $500.00 in his pocket. "Hustlers" are sweating and getting their shoes dirty and are not really concerned what it look like. A female that dance must be comfortable walking around half nude and sometimes totally nude (depending on the club) in front of strangers for eight to ten hours a day, everyday. Being able to dance is always a benefit but not a necessity. You would not believe how many exotic dancers that can not dance but make up for it through personality, beauty, conning, scamming and out right lying. Those are the requirements; otherwise, there is no way to last. She surely can't tell every customer her real name, phone number and home address or hotel room number, and can't tell guys that she is not as classy as she pretends. The truth in strip clubs defeats the purpose. Men are chasing fantasies and dreams and it is the dancer's job to create and maintain the illusion. This is the place where rich men and beautiful women rarely hear the truth. An exotic dancer must have the ability to role play, how she dance is simply an introduction to getting the "real money" her audience is a mixture of everyday society; (attorney's, business men, ministers, husbands, politicians, barbers, drug dealers, painters, her sister husband's cousin) may see her "stripping", her job is to manipulate every single one of them. And even must have a stable lie for the mom, husband, boyfriend, roommate or any subject she must reveal her absences or secrets from.

Why are Gentleman (Strip) Clubs so popular?

Gentleman clubs are popular because of more than one reason; "stripping" is on the rise along with unemployment. You will find older women "dressed out" in the strip club right now. There are females buying stilettos for their first time ever at 35 and 38 years old with their 18 year old daughters also being introduced to the business. Depending on which club, you may find dancers in their fifties. Again, dancing is the least worry. Some of these older dancers just happen to know the place to be to arrange "business" for later that evening.

Bootleggers are realizing that guys are in strip clubs and, the "strip club" is one of the only places in America where men and women just go and give money away (besides church). The dancers are getting lots of money for, acting, lying and things she was doing for free before the economy took a dive, and she started dancing.

The biggest flat screens that you ever want to see is hanging in a lot of strip clubs and the channel don't hardly change from the sports channels, so, a dark candle lit room with alcohol, beautiful women, music and sports, Somebody involved with the club is going to get paid because a customer will be there. It's like he's going to a fair, amusement park, casino or a liquor house to gamble; he has no idea if he will leave with a dime.

Music videos certainly have a lot to do with the popularity of strip clubs and is attracting the younger females to "the life" the glamour is an attraction for the younger females, living conditions and family structure plays a part. Some of the younger females feel like local celebrities because of the acceptance they receive from so many men while their clothes are off, as well as acceptance of their peers and co-workers.

The Hip-Hop music and videos also has an affect on the younger men and as soon as they get some money in their hands, they are headed to support the local strip club and shine while he "makes it rain" with $1000 in ones like he's on a video and after a few songs, his moment is over…unless he do it all over. When the ones $20's, or $100's run out, a good "business women" knows how to set up and deliver the perfect exit and the "trick "go for it. She may say "you better give me a hug before you leave." She may even be rushing him out and he want even realize it. There may be no better place for the average man or woman to go to assist themselves in receiving a fantasy or fulfilling a dream. There are a lot of college girls dancing to put themselves through school and they spread the word about THE BUSINESS OF GAME.

The more guys that don't understand "game" don't know "business", the strip club is often use as the place to receive status, "tricks" believe that the more money they are seen spending, the more respect they should get. The stripper knows that the more money he spends, the weaker he is. She respects him less with every dollar he spend and actually look forward to financially raping him every opportunity that she gets. The guy in the club receiving the most attention is normally the biggest trick in the club at the time.

This Is What They Say.
Experienced business women are being under bided. The younger girls are being accused of "f***ing" the "game" up. Well, it's not a "game" it's a business. A "business women" will handle her "business" if the younger dancers want to dance and perform sexual favors for discounts they are cheating themselves. Although it does make it frustrating for a female to be successful at setting up a $500.00 dance in the back when the younger rival will give a private dance for $20.00. But a good business woman knows that it only takes one "trick" to make a good night, week or life.

What Should New Dancers Know About the Business?

- Each customer is a "trick"

- When a "trick" tip her while on stage, he should be the first one that she go talk to after coming off the stage. ("thank you-my name is____ may I interest you in a table dance, private dance, VIP room etc.)

- New dancers should associate and identify with nothing outside of money (drugs, partying, and relationships) stay focused.

- Never leave the club with a "trick" and never spend the night with one.

- Don't tell "tricks" and co-workers personal information (place of residence)

- Understand that each co-worker has the same goal; (to get money) they are not friends.

- Know how to be quiet and listen, as well as when and how to respond accordingly.

- A successful dancer has to keep herself away from other dancer's personal lives or drama between co-workers.

- It's never wise to hang-out with anyone employed by the same club. New dancers are like college freshman, they will be tested and approached for sex by other dancers, owners, managers, bouncers, bartenders, D.J's etc. Becoming sexually involved could ultimately cost her money.

- There are drugs in strip clubs, the most popular ones are: marijuana, cocaine, and ecstasy. Anything out-side of getting money is drama.

- It's good to establish at least three or four "regular customers" (men that give you at least a certain amount every week). They are the foundation of her "base pay." She may sometimes plan her budget around her "base pay" (regular customers).

- It's not good to club-hop. Having one club as her command post allows her to build up cliental or regular customers.

- PIMPS ARE REAL.

HOW TO BECOME A BUSINESS WOMAN?
Getting in the business is fairly easy:

1. Must be at least 18 years old with valid I.D.

2. Your shape and body size is definitely accepted by different "STRIP CLUBS"

To start off, an exotic dancer will need a few thong sets to change outfits or whatever costumes she feels more comfortable with, stilettos, breath mints, and some clubs may require a tip-out fee up front which normally ranges from $30.00 to $100.00

Tip-Out: is the daily fee that each dancer pay the club for being allowed to work their. "Dancers" are more often independent contractors, Depending on the club; the dancers have other fees such as tipping the D.J. which is $5.00 or $10.00 per "dancer". Inside the clubs there is little more privacy. These rooms are known as "Private rooms" the private room normally cost the customer "Trick" $30.00 in which the dancer pay the club $10.00 from the $30.00 for each song. If the customer happens to want sex inside the club, he would normally pay about $150.00 each song (4 minutes) he's back there with the dancer. VIP rooms normally cost about $175.00 for thirty minutes and the dancer pays $50.00 to the club. (Fees vary with club)

As with everything else, in life, a dancer must **keep order,** customers sometimes would rather buy drinks for the girls and mingle while drinking but then, only the club gets paid unless she knows the customer to be a "regular" that spends money. A dancer that is on top of her business understands that each song that she is mingling will average no less than $10.00 per song by the time she leaves the "trick". Dancers go to work to make money, if a customer wants to get her to conversate for free or give him more for less then, a "business woman" knows that he doesn't like her much as he pretend if he has a problem giving her money. When a customer really wants a dancer then no negotiating is necessary. To start a personal relationship with a customer is definitely hustling backwards. Once he becomes her man, the option of getting paid at least $150.00 for four minutes of sex is gone, getting paid for dances is gone, in fact, she will really create a problem because the average customer enters a relationship with a dancer while she is currently a dancer can be nothing but a hindrance. He will be in the club more often wanting her sitting under him and not concerned about her making money. Then the jealousy sets in when she lets him know that she has to work and make "rounds"; (check on tricks to solicit a dance). After receiving the best sex he ever had, he neglects his business to be in her business more often. The next thing you know, she has a mean mad boyfriend all over her every day in the club hiding behind the name of "PIMP." She just created a "**chillipimp**." Dancers should put themselves on probation and stay away from the guys that she likes. A chillipimp only has one girl.

When she start a relationship with a "Trick" **The "trick" is on her**. Before you know it, they both start to believe that lie (he's a pimp). This allows him to talk to and sleep with dancers in the name of pimping. Pimps look at sex as work, sometimes being a necessary nuisance. If a guy is a real pimp he can watch the dancer that he claims to be pimping, have sex in front of him with one of his "homies" for money and he accepts it as a compliment. Otherwise he is just another jealous boyfriend until; he becomes a jealous boyfriend with criminal domestic violence charge or worse.

What Should a Business woman expect At Work?

- Haters: they can't be avoided in society.

- Expect to lie, and to be lied to; expect to be treated like a lady and a whore, and offered drugs. Expect females to make passes at her. Expect not to be as innocent coming out as she was going in.

- Expect the guys that work there to make advances, to be disrespected, to be treated with respect, to be liked, loved and hated.

The average income of an exotic dancer in the strip clubs that do not have sex or date outside the club ranges from $100.00 to $300.00 a day after "tip-out." This requires the dancer to be well-rounded on popular issues, (politics, entertainment, and business) local and national. A lot of dancers had no intentions of dancing for as long as they have been dancing. Some dancers comes into the "business" with a plan and two years later, the only plan is still; come to the club and get the "easy money." A plan to exit, always work in the dancer favor. (Seek legal self employment)

Do Exotic dancers Drink or Use Drugs?

Hell yeah, you must understand the environment and the condition that dancers work under. The strip club is a place where drinking is the norm. Customers look forward to buying the dancers drinks and the dancers look forward to receiving them to escape the reality of her environment. Drinking makes the dancers and customers a bit more loose and negotiable. A "stripper" may have any where from 3-20 drinks a day. But not every dancer relies on alcohol and drugs. She is the true "hustler" the true "business woman." The most commonly used drugs of choice in "strip clubs" are alcohol, marijuana, cocaine and ecstasy.

Your Girlfriend Is a Business woman; what should you know?

If your girlfriend is an entertainer dancer, she should reflect and represent you during your absence at the club. This doesn't come easy. Actually, to have a successful relationship with a dancer, a man has to share similar or the same qualities as a "pimp", not many guys will agree to let his girlfriend or wife go strip naked in front of men everyday and is cool with her keeping the earnings of both of their sacrifices; but not being a "pimp" there are a lot of aspects of the business that he wont know or comprehend until now:

- When he catches his "girl" lying, he can't be offended, that is what she is accustomed to doing all day everyday. She understands that he "can't handle the truth".

- He should in fact help her with her ability to lie but, also be sure that she understands that he can accept her job and understand some parts of it but, the two of them is on the "same team" and that she should lie to everyone else but, they must be straight-forward and honest with each other in order to capitalize on the moment because, the dancing is only a step in the direction to save money for something later.

- Talking may not always be sufficient when it comes to every woman, not only dancers, the boyfriend should understand that she has been hurt by some predatory male and maybe even more than once. (Beat her and gamble with freedom or leave her)

- He must remember that prior pain and misfortunes was not created or caused by him. This may require a military style deprogramming. She has to experience a "boot camp" style process. This process may cause pain for both of them until it is complete. He must break her down and rebuild her so that she may best benefit the two of them.

- Boyfriends should understand that "strippers" are among the local celebrities therefore if she happens to see a "trick" at the movies while the two of them is out on a date, that there should not be a 10 questioning session of details of her and the "tricks" previous club encounter. (The trick is the one sponsoring the couples leisure moments)

- Don't hang out with the strippers and their partners.

- Know that, she can't be trusted 90% and if he does trust her, he should not let her know.

- Don't go to the club often. (while she is working)

- Always keep her in suspense and wondering of your where bouts. She may call from the club to be sure that he is still out of the area.

- She should know that he find everybody suspect.

- Boyfriends of strippers should not expect the wife experience from her when it comes to cooking and cleaning. Because of the ages, how they were raised and the hours they work, they mostly are ignorant when it comes to domestic responsibilities. But no matter when and why she is mad with him, the chances of agreeing to sex are still about 98%.

- Do not ever make sexually advances towards her co-workers. He cannot afford the chance of a sexual rejection. Strippers gossip, dramatic, and are hypocritical.

- A lot of strip clubs will not knowingly let boyfriends or husbands into the club where his wife works. If he has been ask not to come to more than one club by managers or owner then, his girl is probably behind the whole scene to keep him from coming in ("finding her out"). She may be carrying on a relationship with some one that works in the club, his friend or a guy that she was introduced to by another dancer or co-worker.

- He should always know how much money she has made so that he can monitor the profits of each conversation or dances.

- Keep her secure mentally, emotionally, spiritually, physically, and sexually.

- He should know the regular customers that come to the club. Notice if she is talking to customers that is not giving her money.

- No talking to guys more than a certain amount of time depending on the action in the club.

- When a man dates a "Business woman" it is always good to prepare for the worse yet know: if you find a smart loyal, dedicated "Business woman" to assist you in life then you have found the best sex and best friend imaginable.

- Don't let associates or friends know where your girls work. Pick your reasons why. Everyone is suspect!

Justification of a Business woman

Until now, it may have been difficult to justify dating a stripper or being a stripper. The reasons vary; excitement sex, revenge sex, the need for affection, sex for money or material gain is not limited to strippers in fact, sex and money is America's Common Denominator. There are a lot of females that would not have her man if she didn't have a vagina and there are a lot of men that wouldn't be getting any sex if they didn't have money. Women that cheat or have sex for money and material gains can be found at your local library, supermarket, PTA meeting, city councils office, class rooms, churches, internet and telephone chat lines.

Again, the economy is to "iffy" for people to be "in the game" or playing games with business. If a man has a girlfriend or wife that is loose (a cheater) and if he has to go out of town for a few days, his girl had sex (before he get home) with two guys that thought enough of her to share $500.00 each with her. She uses it for both of their benefit - what's the problem? There are girls at the club on the weekends and they may have sex or cheat on their man because a guy could dance good bought her a couple drinks or was simply handsome and she may end up staying the night with him, for no reason at all but to "CUM." The same thing happens in church, ladies sleeping with deacons, preachers and married men just for the sake of getting away with something they know they should not be doing and these women don't get any money. The guys from the clubs and church are becoming accustomed to only giving stripper's money. A lot of these women refer to men as dogs because she may have sex with him on different occasions, and then tell her friend that he isn't trying to pay no bills or give up any money. Well he is not a dog, she's a wanna be prostitute that played herself by not asking for what she wanted or needed. But the same females have the nerve to be-little strippers, prostitutes, call girls and every other "business woman" that they wish they had the nerves to be. There are less jobs, right now is a good time to become a business woman because "tricking" is in full effect.

How do you know that she is a Business Woman?

- She always suggest or request money prior to having sex

- If you hear her refer to a guy as "daddy" in the strip club etc.

- Don't claim a job but has money, etc… and sleep all day.

- If you find her with 6" stilettos.

- **Her "head game" (oral sex) is super spectacular!**

- She admits it.

How do you know if she is a "Bootlegger"?

Enjoys and crave sex more than you and just recently begin trying to transform her hobby and addiction into a marketable business. You can change "the game" and profit from her skills as well once you notice that she is a nympho and you notice things like:

- An abundance of sex toys

- Buy a lot a AA batteries

- Has experienced so many threesomes that she is immune for being sexually aroused by them anymore.

- She isn't concerned about the color or genders helping her reach a sexual climax.

- Is very hard to socialize with if neglected or deprived of sex after about 24 hours.

- She can have an orgasm from the thought of sex.

- She enjoys giving oral sex immensely

- She will be late to work, appointments, home to her husband or boyfriend because of sex or masturbation.

- She often participates in orgies and or threesomes, and frequent "swinger parties".

- Will perform oral sex on you right after you take "it" out of the "next girl".

How do you know if she is a "Beast" (FREAK?)

- She's overly excited and ambitious to participate in drama, she will even enjoy having a weapon forced in her mouth, vagina etc.

- Has manipulated her pet dog or cat to lick her vagina

- Has shared fantasy or wanted to role play as a rape victim.

- May want to be vomited, peed or defecated on during sex.

Most of these women are tempting, desirable and a high risk of drama so remember to Enter at Own Risk!

(Jamie Foxx) **I love Her Cause She Got Her Own**

"I love Her Cause She Got her own
She Don't Need Mine Just To Leave Mine Alone
Their Ain't Nothin thats more sexy
Than the Girl Dat Wan't But Don't Need Me
Young Independent Yea she work hard, But you
Cant Tell from da way dat she walk
She Dont Slow It Down Cause She Aint Got Time
To Be Complaining Shawty Gone Shine
She Don't Expect Nothin From No guy
She Plays Agressive But She Still Shy
But You Never Know Her Softer Side
By Looking In Her Eyes
Knowing She Can Do For Her Self
Makes Me Wanna Give Her My Wealth(yea Yea)
Only Kind Of Girl I Want
independent Queen working For Her Thrown
(Chorus)
I Love Her Cause She Got Her Own.
She Got Her Own
I Love Cause She Got Her Own
She Got Her Own
I Love When She Say(it's cool)(i Got IT +3)
I Love It When She Say(it's cool) (i Got It +3)

(ne-Yo)
I LoVe Her Cause She Got Her Own
She Dont need mine she say leave mine alone
their aint nothig thats more sexy
then a girl dat wan't but don't need me
lovely face, nice thick thighs
plus she got drive that matches my drive

sexy thang she's stay fly
all while paying her bills on time
she dont look at me like captain save um
Golddigging no she don't do dat
now she look at me like inspiration
she wanna be complaments to my swagg
and everythang she got she work for it
good life made for it
she take Pride in saying that she paid for it(yea Yea)
Only Kind Of girl I Want, independent Queen working For Her Thrown
(Chorus)
I Love Her Cause She Got HEr Own
She Got Her Own
I Love Her Cause she Got Her own
She Got Her Own
I love it When She Say(It's cool) (i got it +3)
she Say(uh-oh)(i got it +3)

(Fabolous)

Don't make me laugh boo
Never did that bad too
Make you even have to
But even if I had to
Ask my better half to
You be more than glad to
When I do that math boo
You always try to add two
I need someone who'd ride for me
Not someone who'd ride for free
She said boy I don't just ride, She'll pull up beside of me
I had to ask her what she doin in that caddy
She said cause you my baby I'd be stuntin like my daddy
And theres not many, who catch my eye
We both wearing gucci, she match my fly
And thats why I, Suppose to keep her closer
Right by the side, toast and to host her
And that she went low so, case you didn't know so
You can save your money dawg shawty getting dough so
What she care wat his cost, you can call her miss boss
I got it backwards, criss cross, shawty got her own"

Chapter 10

BOOTLEGGERS

A lot of females that men meet and see every day at the dentist office, restaurant, on the egg aisle in your local super market, internet or even church etc. are looking for a man. Even just so that sometimes she gets to hear a genuine voice saying, "You look nice today baby". Some females don't just want emotional companionship but they set out in search of a sponsor "Trick". These women will have sex with men in hopes of a pay-off but, she don't ask for money, she just expects the guy to give it to her and when he don't, she may label him as a "dog" or tell her girlfriends that "he ain't hitting on shit". These women are the cause for family break-ups, alimony, palimony, divorces, child support, civil suites and false allegations etc. they are bad for business, marriage, morality and the American economy. These females are **"BOOTLEGGERS"**.

Bootleggers are fraudulent from the start and unless a person is aware, it could lead to dark destinations. Playing with men "Tricks" feelings and money is dangerous and suicidal. These women want some money from their target at any cost to the victim ("Trick"). She wants to get paid one way or another, accuse of rape and file a civil suite later, get pregnant and receive child support, get married and receive those marital benefits or get a divorce and look to enjoy those benefits, maybe even six figures (right Sheree? ATL Housewives); Most of these husbands, bosses and average Joe's have no idea that he is or has been part of a scam. Being so unsuspecting of the con, "tricks" are sometimes devastated, and often shy away from emotional commitments and turn to strippers, call girls and prostitutes. Sometimes this option is temporary and sometimes it is permanent. Regardless of how many men previously broke her heart, it wasn't him; he may have been clueless and unexpected of her past. Why would she mistreat him? That's how some "good men" go "bad." After being betrayed by a "good woman" he depends on the truth honesty, understanding and affection of a "business women."

Listening and reading body language is very important in all business affairs. "Bootleggers" should be able to read the signs given off by "tricks" they are attempting to scam. After close observation and doing the "Math" (taking the known to reach the identification of the unknown); She will know how much money to ask for and when to ask for it.

1. It is never too soon to ask for what she wants or expects.

2. As soon as he starts boasting on wealth and material items.

3. When he first offers to take care of her or make empty promises

4. Once he tells the first unnecessary lie, she should attempt to take him for everything, have no remorse.

She should realize that she is getting paid for what the average female can't put up with, yet understands that she is still…merely a "bootlegger" and is expected to be looked upon as such by offering "deals". Ex. (if you wanna pay for quality you go to the mall or the dealer to buy your pocketbooks, but if you buy one out of the trunk from a peddler, ("bootlegger") then you should not expect to pay full price because it is not authentic). Lies and deceit of "bootleggers" are the reasons guys fight and kill each other. They are the reasons that some "tricks" will kill them. STOP BOOTLEGGING!

Some of these ways of "business" may save you a lot of money and even save your life. Every woman and every man is suspect. In "business," you can't afford to trust someone until they give you reason not to. **Don't trust them until they give you reason to trust them.**

Bootleggers just as gold diggers come with a lot of baggage, shame, guilt and pain. Discovering this on the first impression is virtually impossible, they often hide behind job titles, church or government affiliations, and often "bootleggers" enjoy talking about how well her previous victims (men, tricks) treated her in the past.

Business people realize that first impressions should be over looked, anybody can (front) act once. For sex and or money, a person will give you a show. In the "sex business" men with money will hardly ever hear the truth and half naked women dancing for these men will hardly hear the truth and nobody really cares.

But when "bootlegging" she realize that he doesn't suppose to expect anything "slick" from her. He has no reason to assume she's "in it to win it" and he has no clue that she is not the "good girl" she pretends to be. These are classic cases for the most theatrics and drama, but no matter what... A person that waste your time with lies is essentially wasting your money and every dollar they make you lose because of their lies, they should be responsible for paying $100 dollars for each dollar lost. The economy is too drained for "games." A person that wastes your money is your enemy. Notice that America will declare a country their enemy quick, so should business people? There are many excuses used for lying but if hard earned money wasn't involved, then some lies could be taken as complements because they derive from some type of fear. (A man may lie to a woman about the type of car that he drives, his homes market value, his college Alma mater just to impress and win acceptance from her. But what if they met over the internet and she relocates and alters her life plans because of his "innocent lies"?) **How cruel...**

But it could be as simple as a guy and a girl meeting over the phone and after conversation, he promises to deliver certain sexual pleasures, verbally enhances his size, and performance level. She may drive two hours and it was all lies. Is "who's paying for my gas" a joke, or should that be taken seriously? Women are not playing, good sex, their time and money is serious business.

"Tricking" is a tradition; young men usually turn their first trick between the ages of 17 and 20. That's when he throws away all the stain socks created by high school pressures, rob his piggy bank and head to the nearest, cheesiest strip club in the city all in the name of fun. Just as college guys, men in social clubs, motor cycle clubs etc. Tricking is often taken to be a sport (make it rain) hobby, recreation, status, symbol, but sometimes derives from other causes such as, physical insecurities, no social ability or confidence, revenge, sexual addition, and some plain savage. Tricking is often privately accepted and publically denounced. In some urban communities, drug dealers get their name and identity according to who "trick off" the most money.

A lot of men work hard to attract the attention and impress the women in the sex business. He's happy to have her attention and spends lots of money to show his appreciation. Not all "tricks" have to resort to "making it rain" to get a fine woman, but most men don't even consider it "tricking" some of them believe the lies and sob stories and genuinely may feel sorry for the dancers. When a trick goes into a strip club, he is clueless as to how much money he may possibly give away. A lot of the tricks have wives and girlfriends at home and just wanted something different for a couple of hours without the promise of options and future. Regardless of what any song may say; if a person is spending or giving a "business woman" any money for any reason, he is tricking. You can only "trick" if you got it. Then when it's all gone, you "tricked it up", which equals a "BROKE TRICK!" Bootleggers should be careful because they may meet a "trick" one day that may buy dinner and gifts a few times and feels like he has earned sex and that she owes him. His money is just as important as her sex. STOP BOOTLEGGING!

The thing to remember about Bootleggers are; you can't get away from them, they come in all different shapes and sizes, they can even be found on the egg ails in the supermarket. Some "bootleggers" suffers from delusion of grander (think they are important) and attempt to separate or segregate themselves to certain categories "clicks" social settings.

- **Presidential "Bootlegger"** has the face that you would see on the cover of a "Pretty" magazine and that specializes in dating "big ballers", "Players" and men of respect. She will be one of the best dressed in the building, always wearing high fashion brands and is a magnet for male drama (fights). She looks and pretends to be well educated and well spoken but her secrets are revealed the more she speaks.

- **Platinum Bootlegger** comes in all shapes, forms and fashions may have a college degree or a good job and seems to be doing well in life except, she can't keep a man because of her attitude. She is often sexually deprived.

- **Sanctified Bootlegger** are normally younger females that have made such a reputation for themselves that it seems that the only options in today's society is the church or some other religious affiliation, she's in attendance every Sunday with her nails and hair always on point. Some of these women even move to other cities and become members of a new church and with some; it becomes repetitious. Or you may find older bootleggers in church that use to be real fine back "in her day" and still believes that

- she looks good for her age. She don't really believe that she "has lost a thing" (gotten worse) and you can find her along with her younger affiliate at any club, in any city, dancing with any man, of any age, to any song- every Friday and Saturday.

- **Bad Luck Bootlegger**, she gave up a life of great opportunities to be with a "baller". He "held it down" (took care of her) for years as he promised, she didn't want or need for anything until one day- he went to jail. After the Attorney fees and no money coming in, you will more than likely find this female at the strip club, on the streets (stroll), living back at home with her mama, sister or friend or in the projects living ghetto fabulous smoking "Duthes" and drinking "deuces" trading "This "N" I know…. Stories."

- **Remorseless Bootleggers** just don't care; she has no boundaries and will have sex with any woman's man without thinking twice about it. She will get pregnant by her best friend brother or boyfriend then will put him on child support because she started dating his homeboy (friend). She is really sneaky with her plots until they are exposed then; she is dramatic and theatrical as if her actions and behavior is justified. It's likely that she has been hurt through-out life's relationships and associations. It is common for the Remorseless Bootlegger to contact her victim's girlfriend or wife to inform her that "I'm f****** your man", and some go as far as to write a book about it.

Bootleggers once were called names like: "Jump-Off", Next chick, "Friend with Benefits", and "Mistress"

How to Attract and Capture a Businessman (PLAYER)

1. **Handle your Business**   Sometimes it may seem that Businessmen ("Players") have children with females that isn't so well rounded or is simply "ghetto" (not cultivated). A lot of times, these are the females he may have started out with but could not grow and prosper with. Businessmen don't only want but needs a woman with goals, dreams and ambition. "Do you"!!! Chase your dreams but no-matter how independent you become, always choose a mate that compliments your life style. To settle down with a man that is financially secure is a smart decision but, stay out of the way of need for his finances especially in cases of food, clothing and shelter. Having your own money affords you the opportunity to say no and strengthen your positions. You can wait for the right man for you, or travel to find him.

2. Groom Yourself   No matter how you look or how you are shaped, do the best that you can do for you. Remember that ugly girl that you seen with that "Player" and you started hating? Well do what she does, keep your hair, nails, toes and clothes looking good, represent class with every move and smell good.

3. Don't be a Nuisance   If you have a businessman (Player) that has a wife or girlfriend at home, you have to remember that she is probably wrecking his nerves every day. It is your responsibility to provide comfort to him, make your presence the source of his leisure moments and provide an environment suit for rest and relaxation. Men appreciate presenting money and gifts without the feeling of future promises and obligation.

4.   Be Open Minded   Be willing to experience new things within reason such as travel spots, foods, social environment, type of literature and even some sexual request. Visiting a gentle man club (strip club) with your mate in small dosages may actually improve the relationship. Being there with your mate will answer a lot of un-asked questions and silence the untrue myths. You may even want to pay for your mate and yourself a table dance.

5.   Please your man   In the early and mid 1900's, housewives and prostitutes were the only ones expected to perform oral sex, wives were expected to cook, clean and take care of the children. If you are dating or is married to a businessman (player) and having a good house wife, mother and mentor for the children is important to him, don't listen to outsiders suggesting that you do something different with your life. Your agenda should be to please your man by: having a nice clean and comfortable environment for him, to teach, love, respect and protect the children (family), prepare nutritious meals and satisfy him sexually.

6.   Be Stand-offish   Keep in mind, business men work really hard and may sometimes be a little possessive at times therefore, if you and females "don't get along " and you have male friends rather than females, then you may be better off lying be omission (keeping it to yourself) because what he hear is: I have sex with more than one guy. For a businessman a "Tru Player", you should immediately put yourself on probation and stay away from all male friends that you don't benefit from more than sexually. Sacrifice the less for the greater, take your time and earn his trust. Stay out of men faces with the unnecessary mingling especially his friends. Concerning guys; anything outside of capitalizing is drama! Stay clear of stray "cats".

Get Some Business (Money)

The average female from the chat line, internet, cheating house wife, church going women, knows that she wants or need a financial sponsor but has an agenda for help are bad for business. They are "**Bootleggers**". Bootleggers are not only bad for business; they are bad for the morality and economy of society. These women are seeking money at any cost to the victim, (child support, alimony, civil suits that follow a false allegation, shopping sprees etc.) These ladies work hard to camouflage themselves, often gliding into and with main stream America. These are the worst of females because most guys are so unsuspecting of them to be running a scam. These woman, are normally nosey. These women are a major cause for "good men" going bad temporarily and being forced to forfeit emotional commitments. Some men "Tricks" give females money and support because he may actually feel sorry for her but a bootlegger with minimum knowledge of the "business" thinks that her tactics have worked and she has all the sense not realizing that the "Tricks" may very well have 3 more girls just like her.

Trick the Bootlegger

Money saved is money earned, some "Tricks" are gonna trick no matter how much knowledge or how many theories you bounce off him. There are options to "tricking". The options are determined by: time, privacy, discipline and money. Ex. If the "trick" is at the strip club on his lunch break and is aroused by a dancer, (some clubs are known for feeding sexual appetites) he has no time for negotiating. She grabs his hand, leads him to the private dance area and charges him approximately $100-$150 per song. Each song is about 4 minutes long or pay for a hotel room $65.00 twice a week for a total of two hours while being charged a minimum of $300.00 per hour. By the end of the week, the trick has spent no less than $730.00 a week for 120 minutes of pleasure and fantasy fulfillment.

The "trick" should make a proposal promising to pay a car or house note every month under the understood condition that bootlegger will provide pleasurable services a specific number of days or nights a week. A "bootlegger" may not think about the business of the matter but suddenly imagines living rent free and jumps into a deal. Now a "trick" can have buffet at a much cheaper rate. Some "bootleggers" get comfortable with the arrangement, fall off her hustle and even give the "trick" a key to the house. The "bootlegger" probably kissed the "trick" in the mouth during the over night visits and she caught feeling putting herself in the position of being emotionally and financially vulnerable. The "bootlegger" forgets that a "trick" is always on to the next "business woman". Some tricks don't even want or know how to appreciate "free sex". The union between a "trick" and a "bootlegger" often ends up in some type of courtroom.

A "Trick's" money is just as important to him as her sex is to her. If a female does not feel that she is being disrespectful by asking a man to give her money, pay her bills or give her a loan (when first dating); then it is not disrespectful to ask her for a "little bit".

Artist: Jay-Z
Album: The Blueprint 2: The Gift & the Curse
Song: Bitches & Sisters

"(Let's describe a certain female)
(Let's describe a certain female)
(Let's describe a certain female)

[Jay-Z]
(B***) you know my name and the company I own
(B***) you like my style and you smell my cologne
(B***) don't try to act like my track-record ain't known
(B***) you probably gotta couple CD's in your home
(B***) don't make me say it twice, you acting all up tight
Also diddy like, like, like
You ain't a (B***), I ain't no ball player, you ain't gonna get pregnant again
Hit off with paper, you gonna get hit off and slid off
Before the neighbors take off to go to work
So just, take off your shirt, don't hit me with that church shit
(B***) I got a sister who schooled me to shit you chickens do
Tricking fools, got a whole Robin Givens crew that I kick it to
They be hipping dudes, how you chickens move, I be listening to
(B***), (B***), (B***)
Don't make me say it thrice, you acting all up tight
Also diddy like, like
You ain't a b***, You ain't no better cuz you don't be f***ing rappers
You only f*** with actors, you still getting f***ed backwards
(B***) Unless you f***ed a dude on his own merit
And not the way he dribbles or ball or draw leverage
You're a b***, No ma, you're a b***

(Let's describe a certain female)
(Let's describe a certain female)
(Let's describe a certain female)
Say Jay-Z, why you gotta go and disrespect the women for? Uh

[Jay-Z]
(B***) Sisters get respect, b***s get what they deserve
Sisters work hard, b***s work your nerves
Sisters hold you down, b***s hold you up
Sisters help you progress, b***s will slow you up
Sisters cook up a meal, play their role with the kids
B***s in street with their nose in your biz
Sisters tell the truth, b***s tell lies
Sisters drive cars, b***s wanna ride
Sisters give-up the ass, b***s give-up the ass
Sisters do it slow, b***s do it fast
Sisters do their dirt outside of where they live
B***s have "n"s all up in your crib

Sisters tell you quick "you better check your homie"
B***s don't give a f***, they wanna check for your homie
Sisters love Jay cuz they know how 'Hov is
I love my sisters, I don't love no b***"

Chapter 11

TRU
BUSINESSMEN, MACKS & PLAYERS

It's believed that True Businessmen can relate to the Song Black Republican off Nas Album Hip-Hop is Dead Featuring Jay-Z:

(feat. Jay-Z)

"[Intro: Jay-Z & (Nas)]
I know you can feel the magic baby
Turn the m*********** lights down
Esco whuttup? (Whuttup homey)
I mean.. it's what you expected ain't it?
Let's go... uh, uh, uh, uh, uh
Turn the music up and the headphones
uh, Yea, that's perfect (Yea, right)
Uh, we gots to take and make a "N" wait on this m***********
(hahaha!) Make "N" mad and shit like..
"N"z usually start rappin' after 4-bars, "n" go in
Start dancin' in this m***********
Yea, (Yea) "N" come outta nowhere

[Hook: Jay-Z]
I feel like a Black Republican, money I got comin' in
Can't turn my back on the hood, I got love for them
Can't clean my act up for good, too much thug in 'em
Probably in the back of the hood, I'm like "F*** it then"

[Verse 1: Jay-Z]
Huddlin' over the oven, we was like brothers then (What?)
Though you was nothin' other than a son of my mother's friend
We had governin', who would of thought the love would end
Like ice cold album, all good things
Neva thought we sing the same song that all hood sang
Thought it was all wood-grain, all good brain
You wouldn't bicker like the other fools talk good game
Neva imagine all the disasters that one could reign
Could bring!, should bling, the game, and I could
It's kill or be killed, how could I refrain?
And foreva be in debt, that's neva a good thing
To the pressure for success can put a good strain
On a friend you call best, and yes it could bring
Out the worst in every person, even the good's insane
Though we rehearsed, it's just ain't the same
When you put in the game at age sixteen
Then you mix things: like cars, jewelry, and miss things
Jealousy, ego, and pride, and this brings
It all to a head like coin, cha-ching
The rule of evil strikes again, this could sting
Now the team got beef between the Post and the Point
This puts the ring in jeopardy - until Liberty

[Hook: Jay-Z]

[Hook: Nas]
I feel like a black militant takin' over the government
Can't turn my back on the hood, too much love for them
Can't clean my act up for good, too much thug in 'em
Probably in up back in the hood, I'm like, "f*** it then"

[Verse 2: Nas]
I'm back in the hood, they like, "Hey Nas" (Uh)
Blowin' on purp', reflectin' on they lives
Couple of fat cats, couple of A.I.'s
Dreamin' of fly shit instead of them gray skies
Gray 5's, hate guys wishin' our reign dies
Pitch, sling pies, and "n" they sing, "why"?
Guess they ain't strong enough to handle their jail time
Weak minds, keep tryin', follow the street signs
I'm standin' on the roof of my building
I'm feelin' - the whirlwind of beef, I inhale it

Just like an acrobat ready to hurl myself though the hoops of fire
Sippin' 80 proof, bulletproof under my attire
Could it be the forces of darkness, against hood angels of good
That forms street politics - makes a sweet honest kid
Turn illegal for commerce - to get his feet out of them Converse
That's my word"

Don King is a boxing promoter born in Cleveland Ohio in the early 1930's. King is known to be the undisputed, undefeated BEST boxing promoter of all times. As a young teenager, King was no stranger to the tough ghetto streets. However, King was exceptionally intellectual and was accepted to Kent State University. Having a magnetic attraction to money, King dropped out of college and shortly became involved in illegal gambling and open up gambling houses. From 1950-1971, King had respect as a gansta and a business man, his resume was high school, college, gambling, 2 murders, and a little prison time.

Don King himself must have struggled believing always of his unimaginable success. King has lived through and over-came odds, obstacles, impediments, lawsuits, false allegations, rumors and lots of expected and unexpected bullshit while remaining patriotic, motivational, true to business, successful and happily married.

After being released from prison, King believed in himself like no one else could ever. In the early 1970's, King negotiated a boxing promotion between Muhammad Ali and George Forman with a then record pursue (pay off) of 10 million dollars. The fight was to be held in Zaire and was titled "The Rumble in the Jungle". A year later, King would be responsible for doing something else that made sense; he promoted a Muhammad Ali and Joe Frasier fight to be hosted in the Philippines and was called the "Thrilla in Manilla".

In 1984, Don King step outside of the boxing ring when he promoted The Jacksons reunion "Victory Tour". Don King has been the recipient of long list of awards, honors, host and BIG CHECKS, The list include:

- Man of the year award (NAACP)

- George Herbert Walker Bush Award (Presidents Inaugural Committee)

- Citation for Outstanding Support and Service (U.S. Olympic Committee)

- Promoter of the year (North America Boxing Federation)

- Inducted in Boxing Hall of Fame

- Established his own television network

- First promoter to sell a package to close circuit T.V., paid television as well as network television

- Don King Productions has made nearly 1000 fighters millionaires.

- King is the first and only promoter to have 5 world championships fights on the same card 4 times in less than 2 years

- Assisted Mike Tyson in making 120 million dollars in less than 2 years

Remaining patriotic and loving America, King endorsed George W. Bush during the 2004 presidential election and again in 2008 by waging his support for now President Barack Obama Also in 2008, King was inducted into the Gaming Hall of Fame which is the highest honor of the American Gaming Association.

Don King is a prime and perfect example of believing in yourself, hard work, determination, dedication, never quitting, "wit, grit and bullshit", is proof of unimaginable success "Only in America".

50 Cent (Curtis Jackson) was born in the mid 70's. By eight years old his mother had been killed and "Fiddy" was to be raised by his grandparents. As an early teen, Fiddy gravitated toward the drug induced blocks of South Jamaica Queens as a drug dealer. From the late 1980's until the mid 1990's, Fiddy has "put in work" (became known) and was legitimately in the drug business. Though Fiddy was married to the streets, he was seeking a better, more meaningful relationship and started flirting with the rap game (business). Ultimately, Fiddy would decide to divorce the streets and exclusively date rap and the hip-hop industry. Sometimes, "the streets" can be overly dramatic when you try to leave them and react in a destructive manner. This was certainly the case concerning Fiddy. For whatever reason, "the streets" wanted 50 cent, (Curtis Jackson) dead. Sometimes in life, the sacrifice is worth the reward. Record labels were having trouble believing that Fiddy would bring the street elements into the recording studio and separating the two.

An opportunity came for Fiddy to shoot a video with "Destiny's Child" for a song called "Thug Love", this would have been his first single unfortunately, 3 days prior, 50 cent was shot 9 times. The shooting caused tension between 50 cent and Columbia Records. 50 Cent made a deal with Track masters to rhyme over a remix of J-Lo's song "I'm Gonna Be Alright" It's rumored that lies and politics from Fiddy's rivals had a major role in getting 50 cent cut from the track. Being on that track would have been a great launching pad for 50 cent at the time. Fiddy did not give- up or feel sorry for himself, he kept working and believing until Eminem heard and started to believe in Fiddy as well. Fiddy eventually signed with Eminem at Interscope Records. After linking up with Eminem and Dr. Dre, the life that Curtis Jackson had grown to love, hate, regret and embrace would soon become a thing of the past. Yet Fiddy would find himself in situations dealing with past street associates, bootleggers, labels and other platinum selling artist trying to "see him" (hurt) physically.

Fiddy eventually had to go a step further and start looking out for himself without being selfish. For success sake, Fiddy had to put distance between himself and some of his lifelong associates. That was a very important business decision because being a high profile celebrity, not only did his actions reflect on him but he would also have to explain the actions of his associates and now when you see 50 cent, you don't see 40 more guys behind him with bullet proof vest on. Leaving certain friends or associates behind may have saved Fiddy's rap career as well as his life.

50 cent (Curtis Jackson) is a lethal combination of street sense, business sense and "deep pockets", to bet against him or to start or continue any lyrical "beef" with him has proven to by lyrical and financial suicide Ja Rule, Smurf, Young buck, Rick Ross or Shaniqua Tompkins, (the mother of Curtis son). Ms. Tompkins requested to take 50 cent to court to receive more money for child support on top of the 25,000 a month she was already receiving while she and their son lived in a nice house in a nice neighborhood that Fiddy purchased. As a result of the court hearing, Shaniqua Tompkins will not get the $25,000 a month for child support; instead, she will be receiving under $7,000 a month.

However, family court was not Curtis Jackson first time in a court room. In 1994, Fiddy arrested twice and sentenced to serve his time by doing 7 months in a youth "shock incarceration" boot camp. By 1998, Curtis Jackson was merely a high school drop-out that earned his GED while in "the system" and was now the father of a baby boy. By 2001, Fiddy had paid back to the streets as well as the legal system; in 2001 he was released from parole. This was the time when Curtis believed in Curtis the way no one else could have ever. From 2001-2003, Fiddy had to work and hustle vigorously on his rap skills and connections while maintaining beefs with gansters, rappers and labels. In 2003 he released his debut album "Get Rich or Die Trying". By 2005, the debut album was certified platinum 7 times by the RIAA. Interscope gave 50 cent his own label; that was the birth of G-Unit records. Soon after, Fiddy started paying closer attention to, and flirting with a girl name "success", with her; they gave birth to G-Unit films, G-Unit clothing and G-Unit foundation. Since then, 50 cent has:

- Been named with "100 people in Hollywood You Need to Know"

- #8 on Forbes Magazine with a then estimated earnings of 33 million that year.

- Published A Memoir "From Pieces To Weight"

- Released a semi-Autobiographical Film: "Get Rich or Die Trying"

- Started Cheetah Vision. A film production company

- Received a key to the city of Bridgeport, Connecticut and officially made the day "50 cent, Curtis Jackson Day"

Since Fiddy have been released from jail and off parole, he has definitely had his battles even as close of range as his baby mother. There is no worse enemy to have than a former friend or lover. Looking out for himself without being selfish, Fiddy has sold over 21 million CD's between "Get Rich or Die Trying" and "The Massacre" along with book deals, vitamin water deals and others, it is rumored that 50 cent has made and is worth at least 200 million dollars or more.

Ice Cube (O'Shea Jackson) born in the late 1960's in Los Angeles California into a working class family and has never been intellectually shy. O'Shea was not as familiar with the details of street crimes or gangs as an early teen. O'Shea became more interested in writing and rapping around the time he reached the ninth grade, shortly after, O'Shea formed a rap group and started performing at parties that was organized by Andre Young "Dr. Dre". Writing and rapping transformed O'Shea Jackson to "Ice Cube". Eventually, Ice Cube and Dr. Dre would link up with Eric Wright "Eazy-E" and together they co-found the rap group N.W.A (Niggas with Attitudes) Ice Cube continued high school upon graduation and before becoming a full-time rapper, "Cube" attended and graduated from Phoenix Institute of Technology after a one year degree in Architectural Drafting in 1988. With a degree "Cube" headed back to Los Angeles and re-connected with his group "N.W.A." and within a few months N.W.A. released its break-through album, Straight Outta Compton. It didn't take "Cube" very long to recognize that he had put in more time, effort and creativity than the money he was initially paid. Even though, an agreement was made after negotiations, "Cube" still left the group to reach his fullest potential as a solo artist. "Cube" formed his own label, "Street Knowledge" and introduced a young female rapper to the rap industry by the name Yo-Yo and produced her album in 1990. By 1991, Cube had released two albums and made his acting debut in a John Singleton movie "Boyz N' The Hood". John Singleton shared a bit of advice with "Cube", "if you can write a record you can write a movie" on the "strength" (with the knowledge) of that, Cube would continue rapping, landing acting roles and eventually created, structured and formed a movie production company, "Cube Vision". Cube Vision brought America "Ice Cubes" first movie that he wrote, produced, starred in and introduced celebrities to the big screen such as F. Gary Gray and comedian Chris Tucker. The investment for the film was under 4 million dollars and the movie has since grossed more than 80 million dollars. Cube also had success with the sales "War & Peace Vol. 2". Ice Cube has kept his distance from negativity, works hard, listens, and benefits from knowledge. Since 1991, "Cube" has been involved in at least 25 movies and 9 music CD's while remaining successfully married with four children since 1992.

Steadman Graham was born and started dating Oprah Winfrey. Enough said! (Wink) That's such an understatement of the man; Steadman Graham was born in the early 1950's in Whitesboro, N.J. into a working class family. Steadman's light-colored skin was one of his earlier challenges; he was often-times, too light-skinned to be accepted by some blacks and too dark-skinned to be accepted by some whites.

After high school, Steadman received a B.A. from Hardin-Simmons University and received his M.A. from Ball State University where he was known for having and displaying his skills on the basketball court, even playing in the European League. Steadman has quit an impressive resume; found and directed Athletes against Drugs (AAD), director of Forum for sport and event Management and Marketing at George Washington University, the author of at least 4 self help/sports management books, formed S. Graham and Associates, (management and consulting firm) and has focused a lot of time on the issue of empowering the black youth, Steadman is also a public speaker with a liberating message. Here is a quote by Steadman Graham, "The future of this country depends upon what we give back to our youth and community, and we should always build with the desire of bringing someone else along to share in success", Steadman was also quoted saying **"to get them to realize it's not about race"** or blame but about **"taking control of your own life, changing the way you think, creating opportunities in excellence and improving the quality of your life and your family's, I'll have accomplished something. "**

Of course Steadman Graham is a "Player" for dating Oprah Winfrey along with his loyalty to himself. By dating Oprah, he could probably have almost any woman in America. Getting Oprah may seem to be easier than keeping her. Steadman must turn down 100's of flirtatious passes at him. He has always represented Oprah, himself and the character of a smart, honest working business man and father. Steadman Graham has earned numerous awards including the Southern Christian Leadership Conference's Drum Major for Justice Award, and the President's Award for Excellence from Lincoln University along with Winston-Salem North Carolina, offered him a key to the city and Coker College awarded him and honorary doctorate in Humanities. Oh yea, Steadman Graham is also wealthy, he earns about $10,000 to $15,000 each speech.

Shawn Carter "Jay-Z" was born in Brooklyn, New York, raised in Marcy Projects. Like so many other youth teens, Jay-Z's mother and father separated leaving him with premature contemplations of the urgency and need to "stack paper" (earn money). Once Jay-Z decided to rap in the streets as a teenager, it didn't take long before his name was becoming familiar, (locally) at that time, he was known as "Jazzy". Making rap reality or flipping reality into rap, Jay-Z also experienced the other sides of the street hustle as well.

Through friends, connections and experience, Jay-Z learned how to maneuver in the rap industry and what moves to take or not take. Jay-Z along with the right, friends, associates, business partners and Priority Records; came the birth of his own label (Roc-a-Fella Records) in 1996. With no hesitation, Jay-Z released his first album Reasonable Doubt, which became a classic with 4 hit singles. In 1997 Jay-Z released In My Life Time Vol.1. In 1998 he released Vol. 2 Hard Knock Life (won Grammy for Best Rap Album). Again in 1999 he released Life and Times of S. Carter, the album Dynasty ROC la Familia was released in 2000. In 1996, Jay-Z brought the young sexy rapper "Foxy Brown" onto the scene and in 2000 he did the same thing with the "Dynasty" album, he introduced rappers and producers such as "Memphis Bleek", "Free way", "Beanie Siegel", "Neptunes", "Amir", "Just Blaze" and Kanye West. Jay-Z still in 5th gear and full speed ahead, released yet another album in 2001 called The Blueprint and also in 2001, he worked with the roots to complete an unplugged album. In 2002, he linked up with R. Kelly to do the Best of Both Worlds album. Then again in 2002 a double album the Blueprint 2: The Gift & the Curse. In 2003, he featured on tracks with R&B singer Beyonce' Knowles (his then girlfriend, wearing his chain) and the Neptunes, both singles hit the charts. Then suddenly Jay-Z announced his retirement and began a farewell tour in 2004 that "popped off" (started) at Madison Square Garden and was documented for the Fade to Black DVD. In 2003, The Black Album was released. Collision Course was also released in 2004. After the tour, Jay-Z was offered and accepted the role as president of Def Jam Records. Jay-Z's talent search would introduce new talents to the label such as: Rihanna, Young Jeezy, Bobby Valentino and Teairra Mari. Like all great boxers or athletes, Jay-Z came out of retirement from rapping in 2005 for the I Declare War concert in New York. Uncommonly, Jay-Z was the aggressor in a peace making move towards Nas and maturely Nas (rapper) chose peace and their "beef" (problems) was over. By 2006, Jay-Z was releasing the album Kingdom Come, and another album 2007 called American Gangster. Since his dad left his mom and he resorted to the streets, "pen and paper" and dependency upon himself, he has since acquired and accomplished MTV Video Music Award, Best rap video, One of MTV's greatest MC's of all time, **HAS AVOIDED UNNECCESSARY LEGAL SITUATIONS**, former CEO of Def Jam Recordings and ROC-a-Fella Records, Co-owner of the 40/40 club, Co-owner of the New Jersey Nets, Jay-Z has been known for successfully negotiating 100 million dollar business deals and is one of the most financially successful hip hop artist and entrepreneurs in America. He has sold over 26 million units in the United States alone, and as of April 2008, he married Beyonce' Knowles Carter, the hottest chick in the game is now wearing his **ring**. It's been said that Jay-Z has made at least 500 million dollars.

Jay-Z lyrics can be used as a source of inspiration and motivation to business people as well as "Tricks" and "Bootleggers" (knowledge is power)

The following is a quote from Jay-Z off the album Kingdom Come from the song "Trouble" beginning at the second verse of the song.

"I done got in trouble again....
I try to pretend that I'm different, but in the end we're all the same
I done got in trouble again....
I pray to God, "Father forgive a "n", I'm never gonna change."
I done got in trouble again....
I try to pretend that I'm different, but in the end we're all the same
I done got in trouble again....
I pray to God, "Father forgive a "n", I'm never gonna change."

Smellin' like Patron, singin' dirty rap songs
Tiptoeing in the crib like six in the morn
Everyday its the same,
I said in Blueprint that I'll never change
Its just a part of the game
Respect me, I'm a thug
I might cool out for a sec, but expect me to bug, its in my blood
But if my chick leave me, she gon' leave me for something
She gon leave me cause-a Halle She ain't gon leave me for nothing!
Picture me getting a nut with somethin' sleazy
Somethin'-somethin' so easy
You can take out a speed like nuttin' somethin'
Soon as you finish cuttin', you like "Leave me, please"
Not me, I need Angelina Jolieezy comfort
So I ain't gon make a move unless I got a plan, B
That'll happen the day I have a baby by "Free"
Not to say that anything is wrong with "Free"

Just to say that ain't nothin' wrong with me
If my hand's in the cookie jar, know one thing:
I'ma take the cookie, not leave my ring
If my hand's in the cookie jar, know one thing:
I'ma take…(laughs) ya'll know what I mean

I done got in trouble again….
I try to pretend that I'm different, but in the end we're all the same
I done got in trouble again….
I pray to God, "Father forgive a "n", I'm never gonna change."
I done got in trouble again….
I try to pretend that I'm different, but in the end we're all the same
I done got in trouble again….
I pray to God, "Father forgive a "n", I'm never gonna change."

You lil "n"s ain't deep, you dumb
You "n"s ain't gangsta, you gum
I chew lil "n"s
Hock-tphew spew lil "n"s
I can only view lil "n"s like lil "n"s
But in lieu of lil "n"s
Tryin' to play that boy,
I ptoo-ptoo lil "n"s with the latest toy
Unlike you lil "n"a, I'm a grown ass man
Big shoes to fill, "n", grown ass pants
Prolly hustled with ya pops, go ask ya parents
Its apparent ya'll staring at a legend
Who put a few lil "n"s in they place before
Trying to eat without saying they "Grace" before
Blasphemous bastard, get your faith restored
Ya'll viewin' ya'll version of the Lord
God MC lil "n", applaud or
Forever burn in the fire that I spit at ya'll
I rebuke you, little "n"!
The meek shall inherit, I ROOF you little "n"
I'm a project terrorist
CUTE you little "n"s think you in my class
Substitute lil "n"s who feel my wrath
I mute you little "n"
You a lil "n"- I child abuse you lil "n"
I'm a ill 'n'
Now shoo! You lil "n"s go somewhere and play
Cause the day I lose to you lil "n"s? No day!

I done got in trouble again….
I try to pretend that I'm different, but in the end we're all the same
I done got in trouble again….
I pray to God, "Father forgive a "n", I'm never gonna change."

I done got in trouble again....
I try to pretend that I'm different, but in the end we're all the same
I done got in trouble again....
I pray to God, "Father forgive a "n", I'm never gonna change."

    Willard Christopher Smith (Will Smith) was born and raised in West Philadelphia and in North West Philadelphia by his mother and father until his parents separated by the time "Will" was thirteen years old. This was around the same time he began to embrace hip-hop and rap music in particular. At a party, "Will" met a friend soon to become members of a trio rap group. The friend name was Jeff Townes, (DJ Jazzy Jeff). Later, "Will" would meet Clarence Holmes (Ready Roc C). The three became known for their style of comical and society friendly songs.

    Will Smith was never one to be voted most likely to go to jail. In fact, it was no secret that "Will" was intellectually gifted. College was a no-brainer to everyone except "Will" regardless of his exceptionally high S.A.T. scores; he never had plans of college. The trio would record a freshman album releasing singles like: <u>Summer Time</u> and <u>Parents Just Don't Understand</u> in 1988. The success gained ears, eyes, and attention of a very broad audience after winning the first ever Grammy in the rap category. Will Smith did not grow up in poverty however; having too much may prove to be more of a handicap than not having enough. After <u>the</u> success, "Will" may have had more money than he did sense at that young age. Neglecting to pay his taxes, the I.R.S. ceased some of his possessions and garnished his wages after accessing a tax debt against him. Sometimes in life, people must first loose themselves in order to find themselves.

In 1990 "Will" found himself starring in a sitcom on the NBC television network, the sitcom was The Fresh Prince of Bel-Air which was to be built around him. This was the beginning of Will Smith the actor. After starring in his first and only sitcom, "Will" got the notion and had the audacity to lie to himself and make himself believe that he could and would one day be "the biggest movie star in the world". He began studying and doing his homework on what moves to make and when to make them. While still working on his sitcom, "Will" made his film debut in the movie Six Degree of Separation, also in 1995, Will Smith acting career took a "giant leap" when he co-starred in the movie Bad Boys. "Will" had just entered a new world. The Fresh Prince of Bel-Air would end in 1996. "Will" began a successful solo rap career which would result in two platinum albums. In 1996, Will co-starred in the movie Independence Day then Men in Black in 1997. It was literally fortunate that Will had married the beautiful and talented actress "Jada Pinkett" because he had originally turned down the role in Men in Black. With his wife support and encouragement, he accepted the part. (Having the right partner is beneficial). Will Smith learned that he was very marketable after the success of the movie, he reached across barriers like race, age, gender and truth. In 1998 "Will" starred in the movie Enemy of the State. After a few more hit movies and music cd's, "Will" collaborated with his wife to create a sitcom. Will Smith was inducted into the Guinness Book of World Records for attending three movie premieres in less than 24 hours in 2005. By 2007, he starred in the movie I Am Legend which happened to be the largest recorded opening for a movie released in December in the United States. At the time Will Smith claimed to one day be the "Biggest Movie Star", he might have done good to get paid $50,000 a movie. Now days, he is the only actor to have at least eight films straight to gross over 100 million dollars in the domestic box office and the only actor to have eight movies in a row to open at #1. Today, Will Smith can respectfully suggest 25 million dollars a movie plus a percentage of the gross. How much money does "Will Smith" have? Well Don King once said "It is a disease to count someone else money". His money is a matter concerning himself, his family and the I.R.S. However, it is important to know that Will Smith and his wife Jada Pinkett Smith share an open-marriage. What an open-marriage or open relationship means is: before a partner cheats himself or herself by "tip-toeing" behind their mates back, they have an open, honest, straight-forward discussion and express real wants, needs and concerns even if it includes bringing someone else into the relationship. These situations could be permanent or temporary however, both partners trust and understand that the accepted acts doesn't undercut their love for one another or jeopardize their family unit. If a man has a wife or girlfriend at home and another one on the other side of town or in a different city or state and the females don't know about each other-simply makes him a cheater. Cheaters have to spend money and time to cover up their lies, weaknesses and disloyalties. Cheaters cause pain and quilt. True "Players" (Businessmen) is loyal, honest, dedicated and live by certain moral and ethical codes.

Don Campbell aka. "Bishop Magic Juan"," The chairman of the board", and "Archbishop Don Magic Juan", was born in the early 1950's in Chicago, he began his career as a 100% genuine, certified authentic "PIMP" at an early age. After years of being in "The Game" leading the league, and representing as one of the best "Pimps", "Player" or "Mack" to ever participate in the event. During the mid 1980's, "Magic Juan" life suddenly changed courses after claiming to have a vision from God, he abandoned his business women, his income and the streets. He gave it all up; he retired from the pimp business and eventually pastured his own church and founded a community assistance program in Chicago for a few years.

With a magnetic attraction for "The Business", "Don Juan" founded and began serving as Chairman of the Board of "The World Famous Players" (membership includes Players, Pimps & Celebrities). There is a Players Ball every year on "Don Juan's" birthday as were featured on HBO's Pimps up Ho's Down. When you hear rappers and teenagers use slang terms like "Preach", Chuuuch, and "Tabana Kal", they were introduced to hip-hop and urban slang by "Don "Magic" Juan".

Since the streets of Chicago, "Don Juan" has become an adviser to "Snoop Dog" and Gina Gershon. Since being introduced to "Snoop Dog" and hip-hop, he has played several supporting roles in music videos, stage shows, movies, T.V. Characters are being based on "Don Juan" and in 2007, he was honored with his on skate board shoe by Emerica.

"Pimping aint easy! Don't hate; congratulate." If you are a person that don't think that a pimp deserve credit for working hard then think of it like this, you know good and well the work, time, conversation and emotional issues that a pimp must put up with on the daily base to have multiple women give him all of their money. He must be as smart as or smarter than a psychologist to recognize; know how to deal with and rebuild women that may have physical, emotional, family, educational or financial illnesses.

If you have been one to view pimps as "the scum" of the human race then you must applaud "Don Juan" for over-coming the guilt, hatreds, fears and prejudices of being a pimp. Today, "Don Juan" is active on many fronts and is certainly a motivation and inspiration to many in and around the hip-hop community.

The word "Player" is mostly unconsciously and not seriously ment among men when greeting or self proclamation. A self proclaimed player mostly "high-jack" the player title because it's proven that he has tricked a few females to go to bed with him or unknowingly become the prey of the business woman that he feels that he has "ran game" on (lied to). Business men "True Players" work hard, work through-live through and over-come difficulties, prioritize, puts family first, is cautious, alert, choose acquaintances wisely, influences and create success. Tru Players knows, realizes and understands the hazards and down-falls of women as well as drugs.

If you, your family, friends and love ones have all purchased and read this book, the author would like to say thank you, I have paid my child support and hanging out with authors and politicians. (wink) The next book will be better. Peace/Love

Sincerely submitted,
SUPREEM

STAY FOCUSED AND NEVER QUIT!

IMPROVE YOUR BUSINESS (GAME)

Are You A...
Club Owner that need to change pace with the market.
- Your D.J. or live entertainment is failing you?
- You have the hottest new spot in town but no customers.
- Your dancers are "out of control"
- You need new, hot talent "(traveling entertainment)
- Seeking a new atmosphere for your club.
- Do you need a professional, flexible, agile consultant to help accommodate a changing market and to ensure that you get the most for you budget.
- Do you wanna open a strip club?

- **Exotic dancer** looking to travel and feature? Send pictures and bio. to: thebusinessofgame@yahoo.com
- **Trick** that **deserves** to have a **good woman** and wanna stop paying?
- **Husband** that believes that your wife is cheating?
- **Wife** that believes that your husband is cheating?
- In a **Fraternity** or **Sorority** and is seeking to learn more about "The Business of Game" (Q and Answering sessions).
- (e-mail) **thebusinessofgame@yahoo.com**
- film, movie or video producer in need of beautiful models/actresses
- e-mail **thebusinessgame@yahoo.com**
- A model (video) or actress seeking work in the entertainment business?
- An **exotic dancers** with exception **pole trick skills**

Visit **www.thebusinessofgame.com**
Or
Contact "**Supreem**" e-mail **thebusinessofgame@yahoo.com**
(864)553-5910,
Mailing address is: 2435 East North Street suite 301, Greenville
S.C.29615

To order by check or U.S. postal Money order;
Send **15.95 +4.00** Shipping and handling to:
The Business of Game
2435 East North Street Suite 301
Greenville, S.C. 29615

Supreem's consulting has been high in demand, he provides
- Experience and knowledge gained from previous assignments.
- Specialized analytical skills
- Direction and focus
- Objectivity

- Ability to define a projects goal and scope
- Submit detail proposal for client acceptance
- Create with management a detailed proposal to document how project work will be achieved to desired goals
- Maintain confidentiality during and after the assignment.
- Never accept conflicting assignments.

- Objective options
- A methodology to perform similar future work.
- Practical solutions with known cost.
- A defined time frame for project task completion.

Visit **www.thebusinessofgame.com**
e-mail **thebusinessofgame@yahoo.com**
Phone (864)553-5910
Or send proposals, bio's, photos
Checks and U.S. Money orders to

THE BUSINESS OF GAME
2435 East North Street
Suite 301
Greenville S.C. 29615

www.ingramcontent.com/pod-product-compliance
Lightning Source LLC
Chambersburg PA
CBHW052115090426

42741CB00009B/1812